COMPARATIVE GRAMMAR
OF THE
LANGUAGES
OF
FURTHER INDIA

COMPARATIVE GRAMMAR
OF THE
LANGUAGES
OF
FURTHER INDIA:

A fragment.

AND OTHER ESSAYS.

THE LITERARY REMAINS OF THE LATE

CAPT. C. J. F. S. FORBES

GYAN

Published by

Gyan Publishing House
5, Ansari Road
Daryaganj, New Delhi-110002
Phone: 011-47034999, 9811692060
E-mail: books@gyanbooks.com

Distribution Network
gyanbooks.com
India, USA, Canada, UK, Australia

ISBN: 978-81-212-7057-1 (PB)
First Published, 1881

2nd Impression 2024

Printed at: Gyan Press, Delhi.

COMPARATIVE GRAMMAR OF THE LANGUAGES OF FURTHER INDIA
Author: C. J. F. S. FORBES

COMPARATIVE GRAMMAR

OF THE

LANGUAGES

OF

FURTHER INDIA:

A Fragment.

AND OTHER ESSAYS.

THE LITERARY REMAINS OF THE LATE

CAPT. C. J. F. S. FORBES,

OF THE BRITISH BURMA COMMISSION.

AUTHOR OF "BRITISH BURMA AND ITS PEOPLE; SKETCHES OF NATIVE MANNERS, CUSTOMS, AND RELIGION."

LONDON:

W. H. ALLEN & CO., 13, WATERLOO PLACE,

PALL MALL. S.W.

1881.

EDITOR'S PREFACE.

The manuscripts of the essays contained in this volume were found among the papers of the late Capt. C. J. F. S. Forbes after his death. Unfinished though they are, it is yet deemed expedient to publish them, because they relate for the most part to a department of philology in which the student has little light to guide him, and in which any the smallest addition to our present knowledge may possess some value and interest.

PREFACE.

The object of this little treatise is to direct the attention of competent scholars to the races and languages of Indo-China, by throwing into shape the data that exist independently respecting each. It may thus be more easily seen, on what points light has already been thrown, and what facilities exist for scientific investigation.

The author's only apology for attempting the task is, that no one else is, or seems to be, inclined to undertake it. We have several works, more or less extensive, on some of the countries and inhabitants of these regions, with grammars and dictionaries of their languages; but no one has taken the trouble to study the whole, and make a scientific comparison of the parts. The consequence is that there is not a single work treating of the Indo-Chinese races and languages, which does not contain gross mistakes on important points.

In the first part of the work an attempt has been made, by a careful collation and comparison of all existing information, to trace briefly the origin and rise of the principal nations occupying the Indo-Chinese region.

The second part is devoted to a short comparative grammar of the Mon, Cambodian, and Anamese languages, being an endeavour to prove that these three form one family, the Mon-Anam. These races, together with the wild tribes allied to them, the author has ventured to consider, in opposition to generally received authorities, as the earliest settlers in the ultra-Gangetic countries.

No attempt has been made to write a complete grammar, for that of each language exists elsewhere; and throughout, the great aim has been brevity, in the endeavour to give the outlines which others, more competent, may fill up in detail.

The compilation of a work, however small, requiring constant reference to a number of books on special subjects, in an Indian jungle station, away from libraries, is a task the difficulty of which may honestly and fairly be pleaded in excuse of many shortcomings.

CONTENTS.

PART I.

PART II.

CHAPTER I.

CHAPTER II.

PART III.

COMPARATIVE GRAMMAR OF THE MON-ANAM FAMILY.

SECTION I.

SECTION II.

COMPARATIVE GRAMMAR

OF THE

LANGUAGES OF FURTHER INDIA.

PART I.

CHAPTER I.

Object.—Survey of races and languages of Ultra-India.—Want of scientific information.—Races of Ultra-India broken up into innumerable tribal communities and dialectical divisions.—Reasons for this.—When mutual connection sufficiently established, close investigation of accidental differences unnecessary for scientific purposes.—Duty of Comparative Science to reduce within certain defined limits apparently separated elements.

THE comparative study of languages has been zealously pursued with respect to most of the important families of speech in India, and beyond the limits of India proper the investigations of science have been well applied to the Malayan and Polynesian dialects. But between these there is a blank with regard to the languages of Indo-China, which has not yet been satisfactorily filled up. We possess grammars and dictionaries of many of these dialects, but few well-known writers have as yet considered them as a whole. The speculations or deductions of those who *have* made a comparison have generally been consigned to the pages of scientific, often local, publications not accessible to the general public. In many of the better known works on general philology the Indo-Chinese languages are hastily passed over, and are often made the subject of glaring errors.

In Max Müller's popular "Lectures on the Science of Language" all mention of the Mon-Anam and Karen languages is omitted in a list that includes petty tribal dialects. The Toungthoo dialect of Karen is classed apparently with the Burman dialects of Arracan. The Professor recognises the fact that in Cochin-China or Anam there was or is "a native language, the Anamitic," but devotes himself to prove the connection between the present spoken dialect and the superimposed Chinese, making no reference whatever to the relation between the "native Anamitic" and its allied Mon and Cambodian languages. In a more recent work, Edkins' "China's Place in Philology," which contains the best general view of the Indo-Chinese languages yet published, the statement is made that "in Karen the possessor precedes the object possessed, as in *all* Eastern Asiatic languages," a most misleading assertion, as the Mon-Anam family reverses this arrangement, and this clearly separates it from the Tibeto-Burman class.

Years ago the relations between the various Indo-Chinese and Himalayan races were seen and pointed out by Logan and Hodgson, but their principal labours were directed elsewhere, and they did not treat the subject with any detail.

So little has the comparative philology of the Indo-Chinese languages been considered, that in the standard, and in fact the only available, grammar of Anamese, by Aubaret (Paris, 1867), this language is styled "un dialecte du Chinois" (although the author acknowledges that there are a number of words *proper to the country*, the origin of which he cannot explain), and the people he describes as of Chinese race. It is therefore small wonder that the general knowledge of the relations between the languages and people of these regions is so scanty and defective.

Even Garnier, to whom we owe so much information respecting them, writes, "la langue Cambodgienne n'a rien de commun à l'exception de quelques mots anamites et talains (Mon) avec les langues mongoles de l'intérieur de la péninsule. Celles-ci sont toutes des langues *vario tono*. Le Cambodgien se parle au contraire *recto tono*." The Mon or Talain language is as clearly spoken "recto tono" as the Cambodian, and we hope to show that it is only one of a numerous family of dialects.

It would require a scientifically trained mind, with ample leisure, to examine and fully deal with the whole subject of the Indo-Chinese and their allied languages. To the first qualification the writer makes no pretence, and the second he has not. The vast range offered for investigation and comparison in this direction may be judged of by some extracts from Logan.

"Before the second Asianesian era commenced, the basin of the Ganges was occupied by Tibeto-Indian tribes, all of which had a modified Turanian and Irano-Turanian physical character, while the West and South of India were occupied by Africo-Tamulian tribes... It appears impossible to explain the linguistic connection between the Vindyan and Himalayan tribes and those of S.E. Indonesia and Polynesia without admitting that when the Gangetic basin was occupied by the former, allied tribes spread along the eastern shores of the Indo-Malayan sea, preceding the Myamma (Burman) race in Arracan. Some of the Kyen, Karen, or other pre-Myamma tribes may prove to be their remnants .... The Mon has a strong linguistic connection, not only with the Kambojan, but with the languages of some of the ruder mountaineers of the Mekong basin.

"In the succeeding era Ultra-India appears to have undergone great revolutions, which were probably connected in the first instance with the predominance of some of the nations of the Hoangho and Yangtsekiang that had gradually been absorbing smaller tribes, and extending their race and language to the westward. The pressure caused by this advance of the Chinese population and power is probably connected with the movements in the Trans-Indian basins, which led successively to the dispersion of the Gangetic communities, or their melting into more numerous native tribes, perhaps the Kyens or Karens; to the occupation of the Irawadi basin and partially of that of the Mekong by Mon tribes; to the advance of the Myamma tribes along the northern basins, their occupation of the marginal basins to the west of the Irawadi, and eventually of all the middle part of the Irawadi basin; and to the movement of the great Lau tribe from Yunnan, its occupation of all the Mekong basin save the southern extremity, its spread into that of the Menam, and its eventual movements into the Myamma lands, and thence into India.... The Mon appear to have been forced into their present restricted location at the southern extremity of the Irawadi and Salween basins by the advance of the Myamma, and the Kambojans into a similar position on the Mekong by the pressure of the Laus. The Kyens, Karens, &c., had probably yielded in a like manner to the Mon."*

Hodgson says, "my former vocabularies showed how intimately the Indo-Chinese tongues are allied with the Himalayan and Tibetan by identity of roots, of servile

* Jour. Ind. Arch. iv. p. 481.

particles and even of entire words : . . . . the analogies and affinities indicated between the Himalayan and Tibetan tongues on the one hand, and the Indo-Chinese on the other, are carried on and confirmed by some of the present series (the North Tibetan dialects), whilst others extend the links to the Altaic group of languages; the Gyárúng, Tákpa, and Mányak carrying the chain of connection onwards from the south-east, and the Thóchú, Horpa, and Sokpa transmitting it over the Kwanleun to the north and west; the Gyárúng by its grammatical structure exhibiting also marvellous correspondences with remoter regions, with Caucasus as has been separately shown already, and with Oceania as will appear in the sequel."* This would indeed be a wide and attractive field for a competent scholar.

The object of the present work is to deal with the races and languages belonging to the Indo-Chinese peninsula, excluding that portion south of the Isthmus of Kraw, and to show their connection either with each other or with the other branches of the same family beyond those limits, but with especial reference to the inhabitants of that part of this region which is under British rule. We shall concern ourselves with Tibetans only in connection with their cousins, the Burman tribes, and with the Anamese only in relation to the

* "The Languages, &c. of Nepal and Tibet," ii. p. 69.

kindred Mons. A wider generalisation of the subject must be left for more minute study, a better acquaintance with some dialects almost unknown half a score of years ago, and the attention of a scholar competent to tread his way safely amid the pitfalls of comparative philology.

The close observation and careful analysis of all the languages of the Aryan race has reduced the study of them almost to the position of an exact science, the laws of which are known and certain. Its first axiom, as Max Müller states, is that grammar is the most essential element in a scientific comparison of languages. How then with regard to languages which possess no grammar, or of whose grammar, if there be any, we are ignorant?

No better description of the languages now under consideration can be given than Max Müller's own. "No doubt if we expected to find in this immense number of languages the same family likeness which holds the Semitic or Aryan languages together, we should be disappointed. But the very absence of that family likeness constitutes one distinguishing feature of the Turanian dialects. They are *Nomad* languages, as contrasted with the Aryan and Semitic languages. In the latter most words and grammatical forms were thrown out but once by the creative power of one generation, and they were not lightly parted with, even though their original distinctness had been blurred by phonetic corruption. To hand down a language in this manner is possible only among people whose history runs on in one main stream, and where religion, law, and poetry supply well-defined borders which hem in on every side the current of language. Among the Turanian nomads no such nucleus of a political, social, or literary character has ever been formed. How quickly language can change, if thus left to itself without any literary standard, we saw when treating of the growth of dialects. The most necessary substantives, such as father, mother, son, daughter, have frequently been lost, and replaced by synonymes in the different dialects of Turanian speech, and the grammatical terminations have been treated with the same freedom. Nevertheless some of the Turanian numerals and pronouns, and several Turanian roots, point to a single original source; and the common words and common roots which have been discovered in the most distant branches of the Turanian stock, warrant the admission of a real, though very distant, genealogical relationship of all Turanian speech."*

Among the races of South-Eastern Asia, broken up into numberless petty tribes and clans, for the most part at constant war with each other, the "rank growth of dialects" is especially marked. Isolation from their neighbours produces dialectical change so quickly that

* "Lectures," p. 334.

it is an ascertained fact that families who left their native village to settle in another valley became unintelligible to their forefathers in two or three generations. Here, unless they preserved a tradition of their origin, these two tribes would in time ignore all relationship. The comparative philologist and ethnologist would, however, from the common root forms of speech, and physical characteristics, discover the connection which these kindred tribes themselves ignored.

When, however, we have obtained sufficient evidence to connect these scattered fragments with one of the larger divisions of the human race, there is little use in laboriously examining such accidental differences. If a general coincidence in manners, ideas, and physical appearance, together with a similarity in many of the most important root forms of words and in grammatical construction, between two petty savage tribes be not sufficient evidence of genealogical connection, it is not, in most cases, worth while searching for more.

It is, of course, necessary carefully to consider the historic element and its influence, if any, on the subject. The language of a tribe may be affected by conquest, or by close intercourse with neighbouring tribes, or by the introduction of an alien religion; but when all this has been duly taken into account and there remains an unmistakable and unexplained affinity, Comparative Science leads us to classify these apparently distinct groups under one head. This is the true scientific method to reduce apparently dissimilar elements within narrow and defined limits, and to eliminate unimportant and accidental differences, by the application of fixed and general laws. "These (Aryan) languages are for the philologist merely varieties of some one primæval form of speech formerly spoken in Central Asia. Convinced of this truth, we have undertaken to restore the words of this primitive language organically, by everywhere re-establishing the original type by means of its better preserved varieties. This contains the very essence of the modern science of language." (Hovelacque's "Science of Language," p. 182.)

Nowhere perhaps is a more tempting field offered for such an experiment than among the isolating languages of the south-eastern half of Asia, with their well preserved roots and simple forms of syntax.

CHAPTER II.

Enumeration of languages dealt with.—Dialectical subdivisions.—Geographical distribution and historical changes necessary elements in the investigation of these languages.— Instance Siam.—Influence of the Indian religious element on all the civilised languages of Ultra-India.—Schleiermacher's theory.—Diffusion of Buddhism and literature in Ultra-India.—Burman from Mon.—Shan from Cambodian in South, from Burman in North.—Classification of the Ultra-Indian dialects under certain main heads.—Max Müller's tables incorrect.

THE races and languages to be dealt with in the following pages may be classed under four heads.

1. Mon-Anam.
2. Tibeto-Burman.
3. Karen.
4. Shan or Tai.

These have again been subdivided into a large number of tribal divisions. But not only are some of these really without existence, but they are utterly useless for the purpose of scientific comparison. If it be granted that a petty clan of some twenty or thirty families belongs to the Karen race, we are not concerned to know when it separated from some larger clan, and what are the minute points of divergence in dialect and customs between them and their brethren. This might be necessary if we were writing a history or account of the Karen race, but at present we only wish to compare this family of the human race, as a whole, with its neighbours, and care nothing for the idiosyncrasies of its individual members.

The Mon-Anam division includes the three quasi-civilized nations of the Mons or Peguans, the Cambodians, and the Anamese. Of these the Mons are inhabitants of the British Indo-Chinese province of Burma. Allied to this family there are several wild tribes, principally occupying the mountain tracts of the Mekong river.

The Tibeto-Burman division is much more comprehensive and widely diffused. Its members extend from the northern slopes of the Thian-Shan range, and occupy almost exclusively the great Tibetan plateau, the valleys of the Brahmaputra, and the Upper Irawadi, to the confines of the Chinese Empire. It is even probable that a better knowledge of some of the wild hill-tribes in Yunnan, such as the Leesaws and Lolo, will enable us definitely to affiliate these with the Burmese branch of this race. The principal divisions of this family to be found within the British possessions are the Burmese, the hill tribes of Arracan, the Nágás, and other tribes of the Brahmaputra valley, together with some of those of the Sub-Himalayan region.

The Karens are split up into a number of clans which may be classed under three tribal heads, the Sgau, the Bghai, and the Pwo. They occupy the hill ranges lying between the Irawadi and the Menam rivers, and stretch down as far as the Isthmus of Kraw. Lastly, the Tai, or Shan race, form the most important borderers of Independent and British Burma on the north and east, known under various names in their different localities, as Ahoms in Assam, as Shans on the north and east of Upper Burma, as Laos in the central region of the upper Mekong valley, and as Siamese in the delta of the Menam.

Of all the races mentioned above, the Tai offers less points of divergence amongst its individual members than any of the others. Nevertheless it gives the singular spectacle, in the Ahoms of Assam, of a conquering race, which, in less than two centuries and a half since the consolidation of its power, has adopted the language, religion, and nationality of the conquered, and outwardly become merged into them.

The sudden and violent disruptions of states, and consequent flux and reflux of the races affected, which have prevailed over the Indo-Chinese regions in comparatively modern times, render it absolutely necessary in any scientific attempt to investigate the ethnology and philology of these countries, to study first the geographical distribution and historic movements of the nations at present occupying them.

The neglect of this has led to much error in works that are otherwise justly considered authoritative. Thus several pages are wasted in Professor Max Müller's "Lectures on the Science of Language" (Vol ii.) in the attempt to show the relationship between Anamese, or, as he calls it, Cochin Chinese and Chinese. This is like trying to prove that the English is closely related to the French race, because a large number of French words overlie our genuine Saxon language. Yet the learned Professor expressly states, "though admitting that the science of language was more intimately connected than any other physical science with what is called the political history of man, we found that, strictly speaking, it might well dispense with that auxiliary, and that languages can be analysed and classified on their own evidence, particularly on the strength of their grammatical articulation." The result is that one of his most important examples, the Anamese and Chinese languages, fails; for although Anam has been entirely under Chinese influence from a date prior to the Christian era, and has derived its civilization and literature from China, the Anamese language is to-day as distinct from the Chinese,* and as

* Hovelacque has perceived this. ("Science of Language.")

clearly allied to the Mon, as English is distinct from French, and allied to the Teutonic dialects.

All the civilized languages of Ultra-India, except Anamese, have been greatly affected by Hindoo influences, as far as outward form goes, in the infusion of a crowd of foreign words derived from the Sanskrit or Pali. But beyond this borrowed element the genius of these languages remains unaltered. Having derived their civilization, their religion, their writing, and their literature from Hindoo sources, the Indo-Chinese people have lost nothing of their own individuality. The Burmese language formed one of the principal examples in Schleiermacher's famous treatise, "De l'influence de l'Ecriture sur le Langage," in which he disproved the idea that a language was necessarily sensibly influenced by the alphabetical system it might chance to adopt. The Burmese, the Mon, the Cambodian, the Tai have all adopted alphabets more or less closely borrowed from the old rock-cut Pali of India, and also, with the Buddhist religion, an immense number of Pali words, many of which enter into the common language of everyday life. Yet all these languages have strictly preserved their monosyllabic form, and their non-Aryan grammatical structure. They constrain the alphabet of the rich Pali-Sanskrit tongue to fit their own narrow limits, and clip its polysyllables as nearly as possible to the shape of their simple roots. Thus, Pali *cittam*, "heart, mind," becomes in Burmese *seit*, and *oṭṭho*, a "camel" is contracted to *ot*.

It is not necessary here to give a history of the spread of Buddhism over the Indo-Chinese peninsula. It will suffice to indicate the lines it followed, in order to trace the social connection among the nations of that region. It seems certain that, even if there had been previous attempts to plant Buddhism in these countries, the real establishment of that religion first took place simultaneously, or nearly so, among the Mons and Cambodians about the beginning of the fifth century of our era. From the Mons the Burmans obtained both their religious books and their system of writing, and the Burmans again transmitted them to the Shan and northern Laotian branches of the Tai race.

The Cambodians as well as the Mons, while adopting the Pali alphabet in its entirety, considerably modified the characters, making them much more cursive and elegant. The Southern Laotian tribes, including those which subsequently formed the Siamese nation, derived their writing and literature from the Cambodians, whose ancient seats they afterwards possessed.

We thus find that there are two distinct channels by which civilization and literature were diffused among the Indo-Chinese races, namely the Mons of Pegu and their kindred the Cambodians, on the shores of the gulf of Siam. Both these again traced their origin up to one source, the Indian Buddhist missionaries of the fifth century.

We may venture here to point out, and to offer an explanation of a singular fact. The natives of Indo-China, whose whole nature and ideas have been formed and nurtured by a religion whose teachings are to this day conveyed to them in the foreign language in which it was first enunciated, while they owe almost the whole of their literary language to it, have not been perceptibly affected as regards their individual character or the construction of their vernaculars. On the other hand, the Ahoms, who were converted about A.D. 1554 to Hinduism from their ancient worship of the spirits of nature, with their new faith adopted the language and customs of those who introduced it to them, so that at the present day almost all trace of the Tai language and nationality has disappeared from amongst them.

It may be said that the Ahoms are situated in the midst of a Hindu people. This is only partially true. The explanation should, it seems, rather be sought in the different genius of the two religions. The Buddhist faith, tolerant, equal, unfettered by caste, concerning itself with the actions of men only so far as to keep them within moral bounds, left its disciples free to retain and exercise their individuality. Brahminism, on the contrary, bigoted, severe, and heaping

2

religious trammels on its votaries to keep them subservient to a priestly caste, destroys the moral individuality of each man, and especially excites the desire in its new converts to ignore, if possible, their former identity, and lose themselves in the body of one of the great castes of Hindu or assumed Hindu race.

CHAPTER III.

Brief historical survey of the Ultra-Indian peninsula and surrounding countries, in relation to the connection and present position of the various tribes occupying it. The uncivilized portions of the great races in many cases afford best links in comparison.—Chinese influence on all these nations.—How produced.—General era Chinese, not Indian.—Cambodian and Anamese calendar from the Chinese.—Tibeto-Burman races the youngest.—Their scattered fragments.—Chepangs.—Lee-saw.—Lo-los.

According to the traditions of the races now occupying the Indo-Chinese peninsula, for some time after their arrival, the great alluvial plains which now form the deltas of the Irawadi, Salween, Menam and Mekong rivers were still beneath the waters of the sea. Burmese, Mon, and Cambodian legends all concur in this statement, and all unite in fixing a date two or three centuries after the commencement of the Christian era as that of the retirement of the sea waters from the littoral plains, and of the occupation of the latter by the tribes who had found but narrow room for settlement along the foot of the hill ranges. The Burmese tradition states that a great earthquake caused the rising of the level of the land about Prome. There is every probability that such was the case. The Burman peninsula is still subject to earthquake shocks, and the evidence of the geological formation of the country, proves the fact that at a comparatively recent period, the great plains of Pegu, Sittoung and Martaban were still submerged beneath the waters of the Gulf of Martaban which extended far inland, even above the latitude of Prome, and formed deep estuaries between the great mountain ranges.

The tradition of this state of things does not exist among the Karens, and is another argument against the theory urged by certain writers, that the Karen tribes represent the earliest occupiers of this region. They arrived after this great natural change had taken place, a fact confirmed by their own traditions. Soon after the commencement of the Christian era, the shores of the Gulfs of Martaban and Siam, and the China Sea as far as Tonquin, were occupied by rude tribes of the Mon-Anam race. The upper portion of the Irawadi valley above Prome was occupied by various clans of Tibeto-Burman origin, who afterwards united to form the Burma nation and kingdom. The great Tai race spread over the whole of the present southern provinces of China was, about the fourth and fifth centuries of our era, beginning to yield to the pressure of the growing Chinese empire, and to follow downwards the waters of the Salween and

Mekong rivers. About the same time the Karens seem to have emigrated from the north, probably from Yunnan, and peaceably occupied the mountain ranges on each side of the Salween.

At the beginning of the ninth century of the Christian era the various nations had consolidated themselves. The Mons had formed a powerful kingdom in the deltas of the Irawadi, Sittoung, and Salween rivers. The Cambodians were at the height of their prosperity, of which the magnificent ruins of their cities bear witness to this day.

In the interior the Burman race had divided into two branches, of which one occupied Arracan, and the other had formed a kingdom with a new capital at Pagán. The Tai or Shans, broken up as they are to-day into a number of more or less powerful clans, each styling itself a kingdom, held the country to the north of Cambodia and east of the Burman empire. One of these petty states on the West branch of the Menam was the germ from which the present Siamese kingdom and people were to be hereafter developed.

At the end of the sixteenth century, which had witnessed the arrival of the European merchants and travellers in the Indo-Chinese regions, a great change had taken place in the position of all these countries. The Mons, though still occupying the seaboard of the Gulf of Martaban, had merged their nationality in that of their Burman conquerors. This is shown by the fact that even those of the early European travellers who did not go beyond the Mon city of Pegu, only speak of the people as "Bramas" and the Emperor of Pegu as the "king of the Bramas." And yet Fitch has evidently an idea that Pegu was then occupied by two distinct races, for he says, "the Bramas which bee of the king's country (for the king is a Brama,) have their legges, or bellies, or some part of their body made blacke with certaine things which they have, they use to pricke the skin. . . . And this is accounted an honour among them, but none may have it but the Bramas which are of the king's kindred." This exactly describes the case. Tattooing is a Burman and not a Mon-Anam custom. The ancient Talains or Mons never tattooed their bodies, and the moderns have learnt the custom from the Burmans.

At the end of the fourteenth century the Tai race had pushed down southwards, and that branch, now known among themselves as the Tai-noi and to Europeans as the Siamese, had occupied the delta of the Menam river, and firmly established the present kingdom of Siam. The two principal nations of the Mon-Anam family, which had hitherto occupied coterminously the seaboard of the Indo-Chinese peninsula, were thus separated by the intrusion of the Tai or Shan race. The ancient and splendid empire of Cambodia had dwindled into a petty kingdom at the mouths of the Mekong river, and barely preserved an existence against the attacks of the young and powerful kingdom of Siam. At the commencement of the sixteenth century the Portuguese voyagers found the Siamese power extending from Tavoy.

> Olha Tavai cidade, onde começa
> De Siam largo o império tam comprido. (Lusiad, x. 123.)

This late occupation of the seacoast countries by the Burmans and Shans is a fact very little considered by most writers on the subject. Especially is this the case with the Siamese, who are generally spoken of as if they were the original or at least ancient inhabitants of the country, instead of having only arrived there about four centuries ago. The Siamese derived their alphabet, their code of laws, their civilization, and many of the customs of ordinary life from the people whose place they occupied. Many of the peculiarities pointed out as belonging to them are really derived from the Cambodians, and are opposed to the ancient customs of the Tai race in their own homes. One of the most remarkable of these, the singular arrangement of their hair, best described as resembling a scrubbing-brush on the top of their head, in which they differ from all other branches of their race, is a national Cambodian custom, of which Garnier gives the origin as follows:—

"Le Sdach Comlong (roi lépreux) qui succéda à son père Prea Thong, voulut que ce qui avait été pour celui-ci un signe d'infamie, devînt pour son peuple un signe d'honneur, et c'est depuis cette epoque que les Khmers portent les cheveux coupés court, les oreilles percées."

The Siamese alphabetical system is entirely derived from the Cambodians, while that of their northern brethren, the Shans, is as clearly borrowed from the Burmans.

We see, therefore, how necessary it is in considering and comparing the various races of these regions to take into account the changes and events of their national history, as bearing on their present position, modes of thought and language. In this view the wilder tribes of each race afford a far more interesting study to the philologist, and such scanty knowledge as we possess respecting them furnishes the most valuable links in comparison.

But the deepest and most widespread influence that has affected the nations of the Indo-Chinese peninsula is that of the Chinese. It is not with the others, as in the case of the Anamese, the consequence of conquest, nor is it that they, like Anam, owe their religion and literature to China. On the contrary, they derived both more or less directly from India. In the Tibetan, the Burman, and the Mon-Anam dialects we are equally struck with the affinities to the Chinese. It is difficult to conceive this as the simple result of proximity and intercourse.

Chinese history places the commencement of the first dynasty, accepted by European scholars as authentic, about B.C. 2000. But at this date they were only a small state occupying the country round the great southern bend of the Hoang-ho. Around them were tribes more or less savage and powerful. To those on the south and west, occupying what now form the provinces of Szechuen, Kweichow and Yunnan, the Chinese gave the general name of Miau-tse, or barbarians. In B.C. 778 these races still held possession of the country, and attacked the Chinese capital in Shensi and killed the Emperor. In B.C. 221 the Chinese had pushed their empire to the south-east beyond the Yang-tse-kiang, and the Emperor Hwang-ti added the provinces of Kwangtung, Kwangsi and Tonquin to his dominions. But at the commencement of the Christian era the provinces of Kweichow and Yunnan were still occupied by the Miau, Nung and Lo-lo tribes, which opposed an impassable barrier to any communication between the Chinese and the nations to the west. These tribes seem to be more or less closely related to the Burman and Tai races, but our information respecting them is very imperfect. About the eighth century of the Christian era the great Tai race had evidently consolidated itself and formed a powerful kingdom in Yunnan. The Burmese histories mention two great invasions of Burma from Yunnan, one before the Christiau era, the other about A.D. 241, by large armies of "Tarōks," and as this same name is now applied to the Chinese, the invaders are supposed to have been of that race. But the Chinese did not occupy Yunnan until the reign of Kublai Khan in the thirteenth century; so that these "Tarōks" could only have belonged to the races then inhabiting that province, and were probably of the Tai family. The first intercourse that the Burmans of the Irawadi could have had with the Chinese was about the end of the thirteenth century.

The Mons situated along the seacoast of the Gulf of Martaban could have had still less intercourse with the Chinese, except through the Cambodians, through whom probably both Mons and Burmans derived their present era from the Chinese. This, indeed, is the most natural way of accounting for the singular fact that all the nations of Ultra-India, although deriving their religion, their civilization and their literature from India, have not adopted any of the Indian eras, but have borrowed from China.

Garnier says: "Les relations établies par les Thang avec les contrées du midi avaient propagé sans aucun doute les connaisances astronomiques et le calendrier chinois, et c'est là peut-être l'origine de l'ère qui est aujourd'hui la seule employée à Siam (Cambodge), au Laos, et en Birmanie, et qui commence à l'an 638. Cassini a démontré en effet que le point de départ de cette ère était purement astronomique. Le

21 Mars 638 la nouvelle lune coïncida avec l'entrée du soleil dans le premier signe du zodiaque et produisit une eclipse importante."

The Anamese, Cambodians and Siamese have gone further, and have also adopted the Chinese duodenary cycle, which the Mons, Burmans and Shans have not done. There is little doubt that all these nations obtained their era not directly from the Chinese, but through the Cambodians, whose great trade and large ships with sails are often noticed by the Chinese writers of the fourth and fifth centuries.

But we cannot aceept any possible direct intercourse with the Chinese as having caused that close affinity of words and root forms which exists between it and the languages of Ultra-India, inelnding the Himalaic dialects. This connection between the Chinese and these various languages is a subject that offers a most inviting field of investigation to competent scholars, but is beyond the scope of the present work. Suffiee it to say that it must have originated before the different races speaking these languages eame into their present seats

The Tibeto-Burman races are undoubtedly the youngest and last comers. Both their own traditions and their position go to prove this. The path of their migration is marked out by the affiliated tribes that occupy the sub-Himalayan region from the Gandak river in Western Nipál to the banks of the Irawadi.

The progress of the race eastward seems to have been stopped by the early occupation of South-Western China by powerful tribes of the Tai race. It is, however, probable that a better acquaintance with the wild clans of the Yunnan mountains would show that some of them belong to the Tibeto-Burman family, and escaped the absorption with others, which resulted in the formation of the present Burman nation.

CHAPTER IV.

The Mon-Anam Race.

The Mon-Anam Race. — Three civilized nations of this family, Mons, Cambodians, Anamese.—Indian influence exercised on first two, Chinese on last.—Alleged connection between these and Kolarian races.—Mythical origin of Mon and Cambodian races compared.—Want of historic tradition among Anamese. —Early accounts of these countries by Chinese writers, and in the Arab travellers of the tenth century.—Primitive tribes of the Mekong basin the links between the civilized nations of the family.—Garnier's error in isolating Cambodian.—Vocabularies not safe guides in themselves.—Historical, grammatical and etymological proofs of connection.—Marked division from the Tibeto-Burman family.—Future of Mon-Anam race.

To Dr. Logan belongs the credit of introducing this distinctive name for the family of which we are about to treat. With many features of resemblance to its neighbours, the Tibeto-Burman and Tai or Shan families, it is yet unmistakeably distinct from them. It comprehends three great and quasi-civilized nations, the Mon, the Cambodian and the Anamese, with an undefined number of wild interior tribes in the basin of the Mekong. Little was known of these last a decade ago, and we are indebted to the great French exploring expedition, under the conduct of M. Garnier, for most of such knowledge as we now possess.

Two widely-differing influenees have been at work on the three civilized nations of this family. The Mons and Cambodians have derived their religion, their literature and their civilization from India, while the Anamese have, as we have seen before, almost lost their own individuality in approximating to their Chinese conquerors and teachers. Of the three the Cambodians seem to have been the most intellectual and cultivated race, and the traditions of their superiority are confirmed to this day by the mute evidence of the magnificent ruins which cover the country they formerly ruled. The Mons, although according to the accounts of the European travellers of the sixteenth century they had attained in the empire of Pegu a position of considerable importance and barbarous magnificence, never reached above a very low standard of civilization. The Anamese were simply the slavish copyists of Chinese models.

A certain affinity is now generally assumed by most writers on these races between the Mon-Anam family and the Kolarian races of Central India. Phayre and Mason are the chief authorities for this theory. The former broadly asserts: "We appear, then, foreed to the conclusion that the Mon or Talaing people of Pegu are of the same stock as the Kols, and the other aboriginal tribes of India, who may have occupied that country before the Dravidians entered it."

Mason quotes a number of words in both languages to show the resemblance in root forms, and alleges one or two coincidences in syntax. But most of his verbal examples are either far-fetched, or belong to a class of words that seem to be diffused among the whole of the Turanian or Mongolian family of languages, or belonged to an earlier primitive form of speech from which they all borrowed. To instance a few:—

English.	*Mon.*	*Kolarian.*	*Other Dialects.*	
Eye	mot	met	Tibetan, &c.	mik
			Murmi	mit
			Vayu	mek
			Japanese	me
Foot	sung	janga	Tibetan, &c.	kango
			Naga	ta-chang
Head	kadäp	kupe, kuk	Thochu	kapat
			Sak	a-khu
			Bhramu	kapa
Stone	tmau	tongi	Limbu, &c.	lung
			Naga	long
			Denwar	donkho

With regard to his examples of syntax he is still more unfortunate. He says: "The Chinese, the Tai, the Burman, the Karen, and all the known languages of Farther India are known to use numeral affixes; while the Talaing (Mon) language stands alone, and, like Occidental tongues, unites the numeral to the noun. Thus a Talaing says, 'three stones,' 'four houses,' while in Chinese and all the other Indo-Chinese languages the numeral is united to an affix." Now this is quite incorrect. The Mon, the Cambodian and the Anamese may, it is true, join the numeral to the noun; but in certain cases this is possible even in Burmese, and the Mon-Anam languages possess equally with the other Indo-Chinese tongues certain numeral affixes, although they do not use them so generally. In Mon we may say either "two men," or "men two persons," *person* being the numeral affix, as in Burmese, Shan or Karen.

Again, Mason says: "A singular noun in Kole is made plural by affixing ko, and in Talaing there is a plural affix, tau." But the Burmese has a plural affix, *to*, and the Shan, *khow*, so all this proves nothing, yet this is the sum of the evidence on which a genealogical connection between the Mon-Anam and Kolarian families is affirmed. Against this is the overwhelming evidence of grammatical structure. The genitive in Kol is expressed by the possessor preceding the thing possessed, as "his book"; in the Mon-Anam languages this order is reversed to "book his." In Kol the adjective precedes the substantive, in the Mon-Anam it follows. In the Mon-Anam dialects the accidents of time and position are shown by prepositions, in the Kolarian by postpositions. The Kolarian languages are described as eminently soft and liquid, while the Mon-Anam are harsh and guttural. There is one singular point of resemblance between them, and that is in the first five or six units of the numeral system. This is remarkable from the fact that the Mon-Anam system of numeration entirely differs from that almost universally prevalent among the other languages of of south-eastern Asia, which is derived from the Chinese, while that of the pure Kolarian tribes is quite distinct from both the Sanskrit and the Dravidian forms which prevail in India. Both these systems stand isolated from all around them, and have a close resemblance to each other. This may be problematically accounted for by some ancient connection and intercourse in pre-historic times, but can never be considered as sufficient evidence of a genealogical relationship. The comparison of the Kolarian and Mon-Anam numerals will be more fully dealt with in its proper place. The alleged affinity between the two races seems hardly to require further consideration.

When the origin of the Mon-Anam nations is sought for, we are met by singular difficulties. The Anamese seem to have no traditions whatever prior to their conquest by the Chinese in B.C. 221. Their literature is entirely Chinese, and so offers no guide. The earliest Mon and

Cambodian traditions, on the other hand, exhibit marvellous coincidences, strongly tinctured with an Indian element. Neither, however, give any hint of former migrations into their present localities from regions beyond the Indo-Chinese peninsula. They contain no accounts of their struggles with other races who had preceded them. I do not think that this is due to any pride which would induce them to assume the position of *autochthones*. The traditions of the surrounding nations, the Burmese, Shans, and Karens, give accounts of the national movements, and bear out the theory that the Mon-Anam races preceded them. These last, it seems probable, succeeded the early Negrito race, of which no remnants remained on the mainland, and of which, therefore, all remembrance was lost to their successors, who themselves were, according to their own traditions, only savages long after their arrival in their present localities. It will be interesting and useful to compare the earliest accounts offered by the Mon and Cambodian traditions.

The country of Pegu, or rather the Indo-Chinese peninsula, presented in the ages before the Christian era an appearance very different from that of to-day. The great alluvial plains now forming the deltas of the Irawadi and Sittoung rivers, stretching from Martaban to Rangoon, and thence to Bassein, were still buried beneath the waters of the sea. Thatone, Pegu, Rangoon, or rather the future sites of those towns, were on the sea-coast; Syriam was an island; the lower valleys of the Irawadi, Salween and Sittoung, were long arms of the sea; and the narrow coast-line at the foot of the hills afforded sufficient space for the rude and scanty population.

The Mon tribes who inhabited this region were wholly uncivilized. Although Pegu has given a name to the province, to the people, and to the empire of former days, it is not the scene of the opening chapter of their history.

The curtain rises suddenly on Thatone, or Tha-t'hón, on the sea-coast at the foot of the range of hills that culminates in the Martaban promontory, on a spot lying about forty-five miles north of Martaban and eight miles in a direct line from the *present* shore of the Gulf of Martaban. The legendary history is as follows:—

Two young princes, sons of the king of the city of Thubinga in the country of Karanáka in Kalinga (the ancient kingdom of Telingana, on the south-east coast of India), renounced the world and left their father's country. They went to live as hermits on the hills by the sea-side, near the site of the present town of Thatone. One day, walking by the sea-shore, they found two eggs of a *nagá-ma,* or she-dragon. These they preserved, and in process of time two boys were born from the eggs. One of the boys died, but the other was brought up by the hermits, and when seventeen years old founded the city of Thatone, and collected the people of the country into it, reigning over them under the name of Thíhá Rázá. As the tradition places this latter event sixty years before the Nirvána of Gaudama, we obtain a date about six hundred years before Christ for the commencement of civilization among the Mons.

There is one point to be specially noted in this legend. The alleged founders of the city of Thatone were not the aborigines of the country, in fact not Mons, but colonists from the powerful Dravidian kingdom of Telingana, on the western side of the Bay of Bengal. Hence the origin of the name "Talain," by which the nation was afterwards known to its neighbours, although its native appellation of "Mon" is still preserved to it by the kindred races of Siam and Anam. It is not difficult, without any distortion of facts, to read between the lines of the fable given above a true history of the actual events.

The country round Thatone and Martaban, the southern seaboard of Pegu, was inhabited by the wild and barbarous Mons split up as we see kindred races at this day into petty tribes or clans. A trading colony of the civilized Dravidians of Telinga arrived on the coast, and after some little time they, or their offspring by the women of the country, typified by the *nagá-ma*,* founded the city of Thatone. A certain amount of

* Nagá is a term commonly applied to aboriginal races.

civilization spread round this semi-Indian city, and when the first Buddhist teachers arrived after the third great council, B.C. 241, they were well received by the people in and around the city, while the wild and purely native inhabitants of the remote parts of the country still kept to their old *nât* or demon worship. As the native chronicle expresses it, "when the Lord Gaudama attempted to land at Martaban he was opposed and stoned by *beloos* and *nâts*," that is, by the aborigines.

No further facts can be ascertained respecting this early state of things. Probably as civilization gradually extended itself, the Dravidian founders and rulers of Thatone amalgamated more closely with the Mon people round them, remaining the ruling caste, but gradually losing their identity in the mass of the people, until, except the name "Talain" or "Taline," by which foreigners had come to distinguish the nation, no trace of them remained. No Dravidian affinities have been discovered in the Mon language, or in the physical characteristics of the people.

The earliest Cambodian traditions locate their race originally somewhat to the north of their later seats. Garnier states "Prea bat Sang Cachac, fils du roi Prea bat Kuvero, quitte le royaume de Khoverat ou de Khomerat (Xieng Tong lat. 21° N.), situé sur les frontières de la Chine et dont les inhabitants s'habillent avec la feuille du lotus, et conduit les Khmers vers le sud jusqu'au pays habité par les Xong et les Samre.* Il subjugue ces montagnards, s'allie avec eux et bâtit la ville de Kam ou d'Enthapat. Le pays s'appela Kampouchea, 'race de Kam,' (*puoch*, race, *chea*, être). Le sdach Comlong (roi lépreux), successeur de Sang Cachac, fut affligé de la lépre que lui communiqua l'haleine empoisonnée du roi des Serpents, furieux de la destruction de son culte."

This legend is interesting as showing that the Cambodians, as well as the Mons, after their arrival in Indo-China, were still in a savage state, without union or polity, like the wildest tribes inhabiting the interior at the present day. We also find clear indications of that primæval serpent-worship which characterized the Cambodians, and which was undoubtedly the earliest religion of the Mons, although the traces are fainter amongst them.

The legendary accounts of the foundation of the two cities which afterwards became the capitals and centres of the national history of the two nations, namely, Pegu and Enthapatabouri, bear a singular resemblance to each other.

The Mon version is as follows:—The Lord Gaudama was once passing through the air with thousands of *rahans* across the great sea west of Thatone (the Gulf of Martaban). At that time the sea covered all the

* Mon-Anam tribes.

great plains of Pegu and Rangoon. Far below him, in the middle of the sea, he saw a speck of sand appearing above the water and shining like silver. On it were two *hanthas* or geese disporting themselves. The Lord smiled, and prophesied that on that small speck of sand should rise a great city named "Hanthawadi" (the Pali name of Pegu). About one thousand years after this, the sea having gradually retired, a large sandbank or island was formed, which is the site of the present town of Pegu.

At that time, that is one thousand years after Gaudama's death, a hermit lived on the remarkable peak in the Martaban range called Zingyaik,* not far from Thatone. To this hill a *nagá-ma* (female dragon) used to come gathering fruits and flowers, and there met a *Weiza* or supernatural being who had wandered thither from the Himalaya mountains. In process of time the *nagá-ma* produced, after the manner of her race, an egg like a serpent's. This egg was found by the hermit, and from it was born a female child of exquisite beauty, whom he nourished and brought up. When the damsel was sixteen years old she was married to the King of Thatone, by whom she had two sons. The two princes being discovered to be of the dragon race, their exile or death was demanded by the nobles, and the king their father sent them back to the hermit.

---

* Talain for "Foot of God."

The latter then directed them to set forth westward across the sea to seek for the island of the golden *hanthas* and found the predicted city of Hanthawadi, the time for which had arrived. The two princes and their followers discovered the spot, and with the assistance and divine guidance of the *Thagya-men* (Indra), they founded the city of Hantha-wadi, or Pegu, in the year 1116 of the era of Buddha, answering to our A.D. 573. Thence as a centre the Mon kingdom extended on all sides over the present province of Pegu.

Phayre thinks that this story refers to an actual struggle between the foreign ruling Indian caste in the city of Thatone, and the native Mon party headed by two young princes of Mon race on the mother's side, which ended in the separation of the two, and the establishment of a purely national dynasty. This interpretation is at least a probable one. The Cambodians relate the following legend, according to Garnier :—

"A l'origine, les eaux couvraient entièrement la terre du Cambodge, à l'exception d'une seule île appelée Couc Thloc, qui s'était élevée graduellement au-dessus des eaux. Le roi des serpents Phnhéa Nakh, venait quelquefois s'y étendre au soleil ; sa fille Nang Nakh aimait aussi à s'y promener dans la solitude. Prea En (Indra) la vit, fut séduit par sa beauté, et le fruit de leurs communs amours fut un bel enfant nommé Prea Ket Melea. Indra voulut l'emmener avec lui dans sa céleste demeure, mais les autres dieux s'y opposèrent. Indra renvoya son fils au Cambodge en lui adjoignant sept prêtres, sept nobles et sept brahmanes, et Prea Pus Nuca (Visvacarma) bâtit pour lui la cité d'Enthapatabouri. Le roi petit-fils d'Indra et de Nang Nakh monta sur le trône vers l'an 1000 de l'ère de Bouddha (A.D. 457). Sous ce roi les habitants des montagnes descendirent habiter la nouvelle ville, et la terre se sécha peu à peu."

The points of resemblance and of difference between these two legends are striking. They both contain an account, which geology confirms, of the process of formation of the present deltas of the Indo-Chinese rivers. This must have occurred in at least protohistoric times, and after the advent of the Mon-Anam races, for it is unreasonable to suppose that savage tribes, migrating from High Asia, and finding great littoral plains ready for their occupation, should have imagined and preserved traditions accurately describing their geological formation.

In both we find the new cities founded with the assistance of Indra, whom alone of the great Vedic gods Buddhism has admitted into its mythology. There is evidently a close connection in both cases with India, to which the savage aboriginal races owe their first beginnings of civilization and order. The era fixed for this event is with both nations nearly the same. It may be remarked that the Indian element is much stronger in the Cambodian than in the Mon legends.

It is singular that these traditions still held such firm possession of the popular mind that they attracted the attention of the early European travellers in the middle of the sixteenth century. Diego de Couto, about 1570, writes that according to the traditions of the natives the whole south of the Indo-Chinese peninsula, Pegu, Tenasserim, Cambodia and Siam were at first only inhabited by savages without religion, laws or agriculture. These ignorant people lived like the beasts of the forest. One day they beheld coming from the rays of the rising sun a man of conspicuous beauty and commanding appearance. They humbly asked him what he wanted. He replied that he was the son of the Sun and came to reign over them. He introduced the arts of civilization amongst them; his descendants bore the name of Suriyavans, or "descendants of the Sun"; and one of them reigned in Ceylon.

The aborigines of the large island of Hainan, on the east of the countries occupied by the Mon-Anam races, of which they are probably off-shoots, have a similar tradition. They relate that at some unrecorded period a serpent's (dragon's) egg, deposited on the mountains, produced a beautiful woman, who long wandered solitary over the forest-clad slopes of the island (Hainan). A man belonging to one of the tribes on the mainland of Cochin China made his way over to the island in search of scented wood, and met her, and then their numerous offspring became the ancestors of the present aborigines, the 'Le.' (J. N. Ch. Br. R. A. S. vii. p. 28.)

In the year B.C. 221, under the Emperor Hwangti, the Chinese advanced southwards and added the provinces of Kwangtung, Kwangsi and Tonquin to the empire, and from this period the Anamese came completely under Chinese influence. From the scanty remarks in the early Chinese historians, it would seem that the aboriginal tribes whom they found in Nan-hai (the province of the Southern Sea, including the island of Hainan), were akin to the nations of Anam and Cambodia. The descriptions given show a great resemblance to the wild mountain tribes of the present day occupying the interior of the Indo-Chinese peninsula.

The most singular and perplexing accounts that are given of foreign countries by the Chinese historians of this period relate to the kingdom and people of "Foonan." It is by no means easy to determine the exact position of this kingdom. Garnier considers it to represent Cambodia, that is, the *ancient* kingdom of that name. But in the Chinese account of India by Ma-twan-lin in the Journal of the Bengal Asiatic Society for 1837, the description hardly agrees with this theory. It is said, "Eastern India is bounded on the east by the Great Sea, as well as by Foonan and Lin-e, which are separated only by a little sea." This would make Foonan correspond with the Tenasserim peninsula, and Lin-e with Cambodia, the "little sea" separating them being the present Gulf of Siam. Again the same account relates that the King of Foonan sent an embassy to India. "On quitting Foonan the embassy returned by the mouth of the Taou-keaou-le (the Salween or the Irawadi river), continuing its route by sea in the great bay (Gulf of Martaban), in a north-westerly direction; it then entered the bay (of Bengal) which they crossed, and coasted the frontiers of several kingdoms. In about a year it was able to reach the mouth of the river of India." Now this exactly describes the direct route from the Peguan or Tenasserim coast to the mouth of the Ganges, while it by no means answers to the course necessary to take in a voyage from the coast of Cambodia, in which a long stretch to the south to round the southern point of the Malayan peninsula, and then again northwards on the opposite side, must of necessity be made.

The great difficulty lies in reconciling the description of the inhabitants of these regions with what we know otherwise of the condition of the Mon and Cambodian people at this period. The Chinese historians of the Tsin and Liang dynasties, A.D. 265–556, describe the inhabitants of Foonan as of a black complexion. They wore their hair long, carefully kept, and turned up in a knot on the top of the head. They went naked until Houentien made them cover themselves, the rich with a silk garment, and the poor with a band of cotton stuff. The women also covered the head and wore jewels of silver and precious stones artistically cut. Nothing but the head it is said, add the historians of the Liang dynasty, which is the more astonishing, they naïvely remark, because the head has never been considered a shameful part, while what the women of Foonan leave visible is deemed by other races necessary to conceal. The manners of this people are nearly the same as those of the Lin-e. They are fond of cock-fighting. They use trial by ordeal. When they lose a parent they shave the hair and beard in sign of mourning. They have four ways of disposing of the dead. They throw them into the river to be borne away by the current, or they burn them, or bury them, or else expose them in the open to be devoured by the birds of prey. They represent their gods by statues of brass, some with two heads and four arms, others with four heads and eight arms. In the country of Chin-la or Tchin-la, which is either another name for Foonan, or a neighbouring state, it is said, the people are small and black-complexioned. But amongst them are seen fair women. They go barefooted and cover the middle of the body. They wear the hair long, and knotted on the top of the head. They have amongst them men skilled in astronomy who can predict eclipses of the sun and moon. All the houses are turned towards the east. They expose the bodies of the dead to birds of prey, or burn them on a pile and preserve the ashes in vessels of gold and silver, but do not practise interment. Near the royal town is a great hill called Kia-po-cha or Ling Kia-po-pho. To the east is a temple dedicated to a divinity named Pho-to-ly to whom they sacrifice human victims. Each year the king repairs there for a night to offer a sacrifice of this kind. Whatever may have been the exact localities intended respectively by Foonan, Lin-e, and Tchin-la, there is no doubt they represent the countries occupied at the beginning of the Christian era by the Mon-Anam race. The puzzling feature in the Chinese accounts is that it is impossible to believe some of the circumstances ever applied to any one of the Indo-Chinese nations. At the same time, although not altogether inapplicable, the descriptions will not wholly suit the people of India Proper. The explanation may be found in the state of things mentioned when describing the rise of the semi-Dravidian kingdom of Thatone. The Chinese travellers doubtless found colonies of the civilized adventurers from India, and mixed with them the aborigines belonging to the Mon-Anam race. To the Chinese both the black Hindoos and the yellow natives of the country would be alike only "barbarians," between whom it was not worth while to distinguish. Thus the characteristics of the two races would be mixed up in a general description of the countries. These accounts of the Chinese travellers between A.D. 265–556 seem valuable as confirming the local traditions of an early intercourse with, and colonization by, the people of India. It is however evident that these early Indian settlers were of Brahmanical not Buddhistic faith. The description of their deities is clearly that of representations of Vishnu or Siva, and not of Buddha. These images of the four-armed Vishnu exist to-day among the ruins of the ancient city of Thatone. And sculptures of similar character are to be found amidst the magnificent but desolate temples of Pagán in Upper Burma—copies like the temples themselves of those which the conquering Burmans found when they sacked and destroyed Thatone in the eleventh century.

It would seem that there existed considerable intercourse between India and the Indo-Chinese coast in the tenth century, when the Arab travellers, whose adventures are narrated in the "Prairies d'or," penetrated into these regions. In the middle of the twelfth century Ibn Zaid refers to the Malays as a branch of the great nation of "Comer," which, as Colonel Yule shows, can have no other meaning than Khmer, the national appellation of the Cambodian race.

It is singular that even at the present day the Cambodians acknowledge one of the wilder tribes of the interior, the Kouys, as the most ancient stock, and style them the "Khmerdom," or ancient Khmers. Little was known of these tribes of the Menam and Mekong valleys until the publication of the records of the French exploring expedition in 1873. But the dialects of these savage tribes, even with our imperfect knowledge of them, afford the clearest and most valuable proofs of the relationship of the more important branches of the Mon-Anam family.

Garnier says: "Sans aucun doute, on trouverait dans le langage des nombreuses tribus qui habitent encore dans la partie montagneuse du Cambodge, les sources mêmes de la langue primitive des autochthones. Les Samre, les Xong, les Khamen-boran sont de toutes ces tribus celles qui se rapprochent le plus des Khmers actuels. Leur langue est, pour les sept dixièmes le cambodgien moderne; on n'y trouve plus aucun radical malais ou pali, non plus que la numération quinquennale; mais en revanche, un assez grand nombre de mots essentiels leur sont communs avec l'annamite. Les Halangs, les Banar, les Cedang, les Huéi, les Cat, les Souc, qui habitent entre le grand fleuve et la chaîne de la Cochinchine, diffèrent davantage des Cambodgiens, et leur dialectes représentent sans doute plus fidèlement la langue des anciens autochthones." (Garnier's "Voy. d'Explor. en Indo-Chine," i. p. 111.)

Among these isolated and primitive tribes we find, in many cases, forms of roots which the neighbouring

Cambodian has lost, but which survive in the more distant Mon or Anamese, and others which have a much nearer affinity to the Mon than to the Cambodian. It will be useful and interesting to compare the examples given in the accompanying table of the numerals in the great civilized languages, the Mon, Cambodian and Anamese, and in three dialects of the savage tribes dwelling between these two latter nations.

	Mon.	Cambo-dian.*	Anam.	Xtieng.	Banar.	Souc and Huéi.
One	mooā	mouay	mot	mouoi	moin	moui
Two	bä	bar	ha	bar	bar	bar
Three	pe	peh	ba	pey	peng	pe
Four	pāun	pon	bôn	pouôn	ponon	pouon
Five	m'son	pram	nam	pram	po-dam	soung
Six	t'rou	krong	sau	prao	to-tron	treou
Seven	t'pāuh	groul	bay	po	to-po	pho
Eight	t'sam	kati	tam	pam	to-nam	tam
Nine	t'seet	kansar	chin	seu	to-xin	kin
Ten	t'sāuh	onai	mu'ô'i	giemat	mingjit	chit

It can hardly be denied that the roots of the first four numerals are the same in all these dialects. We then find that the Cambodian and Anamese differ as to the rest from the Mon and from each other, nor do they seem to owe anything to a Chinese derivation. But in three savage and more primitive dialects we find further traces of affinity with the Mon. Thus the Souc and Huéi have "five," *soung*; "six," *t'reou*;

* These numerals are those of the old Cambodian language according to Garnier, and not those of the modern quinary ystem of notation.

"seven," *pho*; "eight," *tam*; corresponding to the Mon *m'son, t'rou, t'pāuh, t'sam*." The Banar has "six," *to-trou*; "seven," *to-po*; "eight," *to-nam*. The Xtieng has "six," *prao*; "seven," *po*; "eight," *pam*. The aspirated *t* in the Mon, as in *t'rou, t'pāuh*, is an affix often found before simple roots, and seems to be repeated in the Banar *to*, similarly prefixed to the root.

It is impossible to conceive these coincidences as accidental, supported as they are by numerous others in the different dialects. It is equally impossible that the Mon can have in any way influenced these distant and savage tribes. We are then forced to the conclusion that these resemblances show a real connection between these different languages, or, perhaps rather, they are evidence of a language common to all these cognate races before they became politically and dialectically divided. In this way only can we account for the striking affinities of the mountain dialects along the valley of the Mekong with the language of a distant nation, with which the mountaineers never had any proved or probable intercourse or relation, instead of with those of the neighbouring races, with whom they are evidently allied, and under whose influence they have been for centuries both socially and politically placed.

As regards the more important members of the family, the Mon, Cambodian, and Anamese nations, their close relationship is shown not only by similar vague traditions of origin, and the chance resemblance of a few root words; but, as will be seen when we treat of their comparative grammar, by the whole structure of their languages. Garnier committed a great error in isolating the Cambodian, although it is not to be wondered at considering how little was known of these languages a few years ago.

The Mon-Anam family is most clearly and positively divided from the great neighbouring Tibeto-Burman race. The Anamitic branch early lost in great measure its individuality under the predominant religious and political influence of its Chinese masters. The fortunes of the Mons and Cambodians have been strangely similar. Both nations became the medium of conveying civilization and religion to their inland neighbours, the Burmans and Tais (Siamese); both attained to a high point of civilization and power; and both, within a couple of centuries of each other, yielded to the superior energy and ruder strength of the races of which they had been the teachers. At the present day, although in certain out of the way tracts the Mon language and a sentiment of nationality still exist in considerable force, the British province of Pegu, representing the old Mon or Talaing kingdom, has become practically as Burman in language, custom, and every outward appearance as Ava itself. Two or three generations will probably see the extinction of the Mon as a spoken language, for it shows little sign of vitality.

CHAPTER V.

The Tibeto-Burman Race.

Tibeto-Burman family split up into numerons tribes and clans.—Mason's enumeration of Burmese races shown to be in exact.—Correct classification.—Origin of Burmese races.—Hill-tribes of Arracan.—Their connection with Nágas of eastern Bengal, Abors and Mishmis of Assam, and other mountain tribes.—All sub-Himalayan races related to each other, as is shown by their languages.—Lists of words illustrating the relationship of various tribes of the Tibeto-Burman family.—Inferences as to affinity to be drawn from comparison of languages and other circumstances.

The term "Tibeto-Burman" has latterly crept into use as a convenient designation of a very large family of languages which appear more or less to approximate to each other. They are those which Max Müller classes as Gangetic and Lohitic, names which, with all due deference to the learned Professor, really have little relevant meaning in this case.

Under no other head, perhaps, is so vast a number of dialects included. Max Müller gives forty-five, and this only includes the dialects known and recorded; whereas it is stated that, among the Nága tribes, different dialects exist in almost every separate village, which would increase the number *ad infinitum*. It may be as well to state, while referring to Professor Max Müller's list,* that he has erroneously entered under

* "Science of Language," vol. i. p. 452.

the class "Lohitic" a language called "Tunglhu" in Tenasserim. By this is evidently meant the "Toung-thoo," and Toung-thoo is a dialect of the Karen, which the Professor rightly does not class as Lohitic. Whether it is really necessary to preserve this long nomenclature is a question. Logan has concisely described the process of the manufacture of these multifarious dialects.

"Perpetual aggressions and frequent conquests, extirpations of villages, and migrations, mark the modern history of nearly all these Tibeto-Burman tribes, and of the different clans of the same tribe. Their normal condition and relations, while extremely favourable to the maintenance of a minute division of communities and dialects, are opposed to any long preservation of their peculiarities. We find the same tribe separating into clans and villages permanently at war with each other, Kuki fleeing from Kuki, Singpho from Singpho, Abor from Abor. We can thus understand how, in such a country, and before the Aryans filled the plains, the lapse of a few centuries would transform a colony from a barbarous Sifan clan, descending the Himalaya by a single pass, into a dozen scattered tribes, speaking as many dialects, and no longer recognizing their common descent."*

"Within the mountainous parts of the limits of the modern kingdom of Nipál there are thirteen distinct and strongly marked dialects spoken. They are ex-

* "Journ. Ind. Arch." N. S., vol. ii. p. 82.

tremely rude, owing to the people who speak them having crossed the snows before learning dawned on Tibet, and the physical features of their new home having tended to break up and enfeeble the common speech which they brought with them. At present the several tribes or clans can hardly speak intelligibly to each other."*

We shall have to contemplate a similar state of things in the country lying east of the Brahmapootra river, and along the chain of mountains that hem in the independent kingdom of Burma on the north and west.

The affinity between the Burman and Tibetan races has been sufficiently recognized not to require detailed proof. The connection and relation of the minor tribes to the Burmese has been in some cases allowed, in others left an open question requiring further investigation.

Dr. Mason enumerates eleven Burmese tribes "of unquestionably common origin," and adds several others which he considers as doubtful. They are as under:—

Burmese.	Doubtful.
1. Burmese.	Kakhyens or Kakoos.
2. Arracanese.	Kamis or Kemees.
3. Mugs.	Kyaus.
4. Kanyans.	Koons.
5. Toungooers.	Sak.
6. Tavoyers.	Mru.
7. Yaus or Yos.	Shendoos (or Kúkis).
8. Yebains or Zebaings.	
9. Pyus.	
10. Kados.	
11. Danus.	

* B. H. Hodgson, "Illustrations of the Literature," &c. Serampore, 1841, p. 1.

We may very shortly dispose of several in this list. The term "Mugs" is simply an epithet applied to the Arracanese by the people of Bengal, unknown to the Burmese language; the meaning of the word cannot even be ascertained, and to enter it as a tribal name in a scientific list is like including the "Yankees" as one of the nations of America, distinct from the Americans. It is rendered still more absurd when Phayre derives it "probably from a tribe of Brahmins termed 'Magas,' said to have emigrated eastward from Bengal;" to which Mason adds, "Magas looks very much like Magos, the priest of the Medes." Was this meant in earnest? Next we have the "Kanyans," who are traditionally said to have been one of the tribes that were incorporated to form the "Burman" nation; where they now exist, or what is their language, it would be a puzzle to ascertain. The same applies to the "Pyus," said to have been the tribe inhabiting the present district of Prome, but now as unknown there as the Trinobantes are in Middlesex. Toungoo or Toung-ngoo was one of the petty kingdoms founded by younger branches of the Burman royal family, as the head of the race grew weak, and though the main body of the population was Burmese, it was very mixed, and has no more claim to rank as a separate tribe than has that of any other Burman town.

The "Tavoyers," or people of Tavoy, might, in virtue of a very peculiar dialect, claim tribal rank; but they are only a colony of the Arracanese, as is stated in their traditions and confirmed by their language, which has since become corrupted by Shan or Siamese influence. But there is no reason for separating them either ethnologically or linguistically from their parent stock.

The Yaus, Yebaings, Kados, and Danus, are recognized by the Burmans proper as being the wilder and more primitive branches of their race; but, unfortunately, we have no trustworthy specimens of their dialects from which to form conclusions. The dialects of the Yaus and Yebaings are certainly unintelligible to any Burmans, and the numerals of the latter show no affinity to any of their neighbours. They are :—

1 = tsoomeik.	6 = louk-kay.
2 = tsoo-toung.	7 = thai khan.
3 = baloungtha.	8 = loung moo.
4 = lah-bee.	9 = ngain koung.
5 = hgay houk.	10 = loung-teik.*

Mason says the Danus "speak the Burmese language in a rude nasal and guttural dialect."

In the absence of further information we can only conclude that these are some of the many petty clans of kindred race which the force of circumstances amalgamated into a political unit as the Burman nation, these retaining in a greater degree their primitive characteristics.

---

* Collected in the Shwegyeen District.

We are now reduced to the two great branches of the Myamma or Burmese race; the Burmans proper, and the Arracanese. Should these be so clearly and absolutely divided?

The traditions or histories of both nations give us the same accounts, that, on the death of the founder of the first Burman kingdom, his two sons disputed the succession to the throne, and one of them led a part of the people to the westward across the mountains, and established a separate kingdom in Arracan, driving out the savage occupants of the country. According to this there is no ethnological distinction originally between the Arracanese and the Burmans proper. What is the divergence in language?

The Burmans acknowledge that the oldest and purest form of their language has been preserved in Arracan. This is borne out by the evidence of the dialect itself, which retains the original pronunciation of words which are subject to permutation of the letters in Burmese, and which also uses many words in a sense now obsolete in Burma proper. The structure of the two dialects is however precisely the same, and their divergence is not more than exists between the English of Somersetshire and Middlesex.

The Arracanese and Burmese differ in two essential points; namely, that, in the former, words are pronounced phonetically, or nearly so, while, in the latter, several letters acquire in certain combinations entirely different values. Thus in all the Indo-Chinese languages the vowel *a* being inherent in every consonant where no other vowel is expressed, the combination *k'k* would be pronounced truly in Arracanese *kăk*; but in Burmese both the sound of the inherent vowel and that of the final consonant would be entirely changed, and the above combination would be pronounced *ket*. In the same way *ap* is pronounced *at*; *am*, *an*; *et*, *eik*; and so in several other forms; whereas in Arracanese these retain their natural phonetic values.

Secondly the Arracanese uses many words and forms of expression which have either become obsolete in Burmese, or have acquired another meaning. To instance one striking case. The Arracanese and several of the hill tribes use the word *lá* for "go," while this in Burmese means "to come," and could not possibly signify "go;" but we find that in Burmese this same root *lá*, with the heavy accent, means (to use Judson's definition), "to proceed from a starting place to some boundary," although it is never found in actual use in this sense. The Arracanese has thus retained the root in both its forms and senses, as "to come" and "to go," while the Burmese has rejected its application in the latter sense. The Arracanese dialect is also much more guttural and harsher in sound than the Burmese, which delights in softening and smoothing over any difficulties of pronunciation. This is especially remarkable in the letter which is really an *r*, and is so pronounced by the Arracanese, but is softened into a *y* by the Burmans. The following examples will afford the means of contrasting, by a few simple sentences, the peculiar features of the two dialects, and will show how little difference there is between them. The upper line gives the Burmese, the middle the English translation, and the lower the Arracanese.

1. kyunop-do, or kyun-do.
we we
akyuanop-ro, akyuan-ro.

The Burmese omits the inherent *a* in *kyu'n*, which the Arracanese fully gives. The plural affix is *do* in the first and *ro* in the second.

2. nga-do.
we
nga-ro.

3. nga-do netpan thwa leim mee.
we to-morrow go will.
nga-ro manet-ka ta mee lo.

4. ming bey go thwa mee lai.
you where go will? (Where are you going?)
mang zago lá hpo lai.

The Arracanese here gives the true sound of the inherent vowel in the form *m'ng* which the Burmese converts into *i*, *ming*. Instead of the Burmese *bey*, "what" "where," the Arracanese has an old form *za*, now obsolete in Burma. We find *lā*, "go," for the Burmese *thwa*, as mentioned above, and in place of the verbal affix *mee* the Arracanese uses *hpo*.

5. Ning nga yeik leim mee.
Yon I beat will.
Nang go nga that leim mee.

Here the word *that* is employed by the Arracanese in the sense merely of "to beat," "to strike," but in Burmese it would mean only "to kill," used in such an expression as the above; yet in one case it is still retained in Burmese in the sense of "to strike," namely, with respect to the act of striking in boxing.

These examples display the chief points of divergence between the two dialects, and show that the Arracanese has preserved the older and purer form of the language, while the Burmese has been greatly subject to phonetic decay or corruption. This is, doubtless, in some degree owing to the different social and political history of the two countries. Arracan has been much more isolated, and the people have preserved their race-purity to a greater extent. Their intercourse has chiefly been with the distinct and alien Hindu race, whose influence, though in some things great, has little affected their language or their blood. Burma, on the contrary, has been subject to long and frequent periods of domination by nations of kindred origin, the Shans, and the Mons, and to close intercourse with them and also with the Chinese, throughout her history. The Burmans have received a vast amount of foreign and yet kindred element into their nation, which has amalgamated with and been insensibly affected by it; while the Arracanese and their Hindu neighbours have remained in contact, but, like oil and water, without fusion.

We have thus reduced Mason's list of eleven Burmese tribes to six ascertained varieties of dialect, and it is probable that for a general classification of languages, which does not deal with mere provincialisms, the term "Burmese" should be made to include the Arracanese, Kados, and Danus. The Yau and Yebaing, as far as we know of them, must still be kept distinct.

There remain the "doubtful" tribes, all of whom, except the Kakhyens, inhabit the mountainous country lying between Bengal and Burma, generally known as the Arracan range, whence these tribes are known as the "Arracan Hill Tribes." Logan often terms them "Yoma tribes," but "Yoma" is simply a Burmese word meaning *any* mountain range, and therefore a misnomer if applied thus specifically. Of late years our knowledge of these tribes, and others in similar positions in the north-east part of Bengal, has much increased, and their mutual relationship and connection with the Tibeto-Burman family has been more clearly established. Of all this family the Burmese (including their Arracanese brethren) alone have any literature, or possess any probable traditions of their origin and early history. According to Burmese traditions, the founders of their race and nation came from the West, from the valley of the Ganges, into their present seats, which they found occupied previously by the wilder tribes who are now confined to the mountain tracts.

They even claim a Rajpoot origin for the people, while the royal family pretend to trace their descent from the sacred Solar and Lunar dynasties of Hindustan. This myth has generally been ascribed to national vanity and arrogance, and completely ignored. Sir A. Phayre is quite opposed to the theory, and says: "The supposed immigration of any of the royal races of Gangetic India to the Iráwadí in the sixth century B.C., or even later, will appear very improbable. I see no reason for doubting that they (the Burman tribes) found their way into the valley of the Iráwadí by what is now the track of the Chinese caravans from Yunnan, which track debouches at Bamo on the river."* That is to say, Sir A. Phayre places the original domicile of the Burman race in the south-western provinces of China. Whether he would now deliberately uphold this opinion is doubtful; and, with all respect for so great an authority, it appears utterly without foundation. There seems no reason why we should peremptorily reject the Burman tradition in so far as it traces their migratory route from the Gangetic valley. Their Rajpoot origin is of course an invention of courtly historians of a date after the introduction of Buddhism; but, in the absence of any clear evidence to the contrary, it appears more reasonable to follow the lines of ancient tradition as far as they agree with

* "History of the Burman Race," Journ. Asiat. Soc. Bengal.

probabilities. What little evidence on the subject we can collect seems also to support this idea.

The Burmans represent themselves as the last comers in the country, and state that when they penetrated into Arracan, they found the country occupied by savage monsters termed by them Beloos, whom they expelled; an evidently figurative account of the wilder tribes whom they found in prior possession of the soil. Sir A. Phayre and other authorities consider it as most probable that such actually was the case. We should then have, after the first wave of the Mon-Anam immigration, an irruption of a number of petty savage tribes, whose representatives and descendants at the present day occupy the hill tracts, in much the same state as their forefathers were.

The hill tribes of Arracan are, according to the Administration Reports, the Khyengs, the Kamis or Kumis, the Mrus, the Sak, the Kyaus or Chyaus, the Anoos, the Toungthas, the Shendoos or Kukis, and two or three other petty tribes, of which only a few families exist; but it is probable that a better acquaintance with them would show that these are only clannish divisions of some other tribe.

These tribes, if we allow the evidence of language, of manners, and of physical characteristics, are closely allied to the Nága tribes of Eastern Bengal, and to the Abors and Mishmis of Assam. It is generally believed that these, or kindred races of Turanian origin, occupied the valley of Gangetic India before the advancing Aryan invaders drove them from the plains to their present mountain fastnesses. All these tribes doubtless formed the first wave of the later Turanian emigration from the Central Asian plateau, the Bhotian and Burman races being their successors. To them also would seem to belong those whom Hodgson calls the "broken tribes" of Nipál, the Chepang, Vayu and Kusunda. These latter tribes afford an important and curious link in the chain of evidence, which thus stretches from the Arracan hills far away to the westward, to the Kali and Gunduk rivers in West Nipál.

Hodgson has clearly shown the connection of the Chepangs with the Tibetan and Lhopa races, and has traced the affinities in these dialects in a pretty full vocabulary of the Chepang language. But by far the greater number of coincident words are derived from roots common to all or nearly all the cognate dialects of Tibet, Nipál and high Asia. Thus variations of the simple roots for such words as eye, fire, day, moon, dog, fish, sun, road, and several others which he gives, are common to a dozen other dialects besides the Chepang and Tibetan or Lhópa, and are found in Nipál, in Sifan, in Burma, in Siam, and do not prove a closer affinity between the Chepangs and the Lhopas than between the former and the Néwars, the Manyak or the Burmans.

But when we compare the widely-sundered languages of the Chepangs and of the hill tribes of Arracan, we are at once struck by the identity sometimes of roots, often of actual words, which are not to be found in any of the cognate Tibeto-Himalayan or Sifanese dialects. In some cases the root is common to others of these languages, but the particular form in the Chepang is only found in the Khyen, the Kumi, or the Karen.

Some examples are given below for comparison. There are many other words in which a common root may be found in other dialects :—

	Chepang.	Arracan Tribes.	
1. Arm	Krût	Makuht	Khyen.
2. Bird	Mo-wá	Ta-wá	Mru.
		Wá-si	Sak.
3. Blood	Wí	Wí	Mru.
4. Child	Cho	So	Khyen.
5. Dawn	Wágo	Awá	Khyen.
6. Fowl	Wá	Ta-wá	Mru.
7. Hog	Piak	Ta-pak	Mru.
8. Hand	Kút-pa	Kuth	Khyen.
		A-kú	Kumi.
		Rut	Mru.
		Ta-ku	Sak.
9. Hair	Min	Kú-mi	Sak.
10. Insect, ant	Pling	Mling	Khyen.
		Ba-lin	Kumi.
		Pa-lin	Kumi.
11. Milk	Gnú-tí	Sni-twi	Khyen.
		Nuh-tie	Karen.
12. Ox	Shya	Sharh	Khyen.
		Tsi-yá	Mru.
13. Monkey	Yúkh	Ta-yût	Mru.
14. Night	Yá	A-yán	Khyen.
15. Woman	Mirû	Mru (=man)	Mru.
16. To give (sa=verb affix.)	Buï-sa	Na-pú	Kami.
		Pei	Kumi.
17. To take	Li-sa	La	Kami.
		Lo	Kumi.

In 2, 6, 7, 13, it will be seen that the syllable *ta* is the nominal prefix in Mru. In 9, *ku* in Sak means "head," *ku-mi* is therefore "head-hair." In 11 the first root in each dialect signifies "breast," the second "water;" milk is therefore literally "breast-water."

This resemblance between dialects separated by so great a distance geographically, and by centuries of time, is surely in itself sufficient to prove the affinity of the tribes speaking them. Hodgson has conjectured that these "broken tribes" between the Kali and Gunduk rivers may have been separated from their kindred and driven westward. We may also suppose that at an early period the whole sub-Himalayan region was occupied by tribes allied to the Chepangs and Arracan mountaineers, who were cut asunder and driven out of central Nipál by the incursion of the Newar races at present possessing the country, some 1000 to 1300 years ago, which is the date Hodgson assigns to this event.

Many years have elapsed since Mr. Hodgson, by his researches, indicated "that the sub-Himalayan races are all closely affiliated, and are all of northern origin;" it would only be quoting from his well-known papers to enter further on this subject. We have linked the western hill tribes of Burma with the widely-sundered Chepangs and Kusundas of Nipál, but a vast gap exists between the Gunduk river in Nipál and the eastern bank of the Brahmapútra, where we meet the next representatives of this race.

Here, in the vast tract of mountainous country stretching from the Gáro hills along the southern part of Assam, and bordering on Manipúr and Burma, is the home of those manifold tribes and clans, of which the greater proportion are classed together under the term "Nága." Here also are the Gáros, Khásias, Kacháris, Kukis, Singphos, and several other tribes whose mutual relation to each other does not yet seem quite determined. When we compare their vocabularies with each other, they exhibit singular affinities, and all that we know of them confirms the supposition that they form but one great race, of which the tribes in the Arracan mountains of Burma are but the branches. One of the best authorities on the Nága races, Captain J. Butler, affirms :—"Our late explorations have clearly ascertained that the great Nága race does undoubtedly cross over the main watershed dividing the waters which flow north into the Brahmapútra, from those flowing south into the Iráwadí; and they have also furnished very strong grounds for believing that in all probability it extends as far as the banks of the Kyendwen (Námtonái or Ningthi) river, the great western tributary of the Iráwadí. Indeed, there is room to believe that further explorations may, ere long, lead us to discover that the Kakhyen and Khyen (often pronounced Kachin and Chin) tribes, spoken of by former writers (Pemberton, Yule, Hannay, &c.), are but offshoots of this one great race."* In 1835 Captain Hannay, with the little knowledge then possessed of these people, identified "the Khyens with the Nágas of the Assam mountains." In comparing the vocabularies of these races, and drawing conclusions from them, we must remember that the peculiar character of these dialects, and the social conditions of the people speaking them, constitute an important element in the comparison. Max Müller truly says: "No doubt the evidence on which the relationship of French and Italian, of Greek and Latin, of Lithuanian and Sanskrit, of Hebrew and Arabic, has been established, is the most satisfactory; but . . . . to call for the same evidence in support of the homogeneousness of the Turanian languages, is to call for evidence which, from the nature of the case, it is impossible to supply. . . . . The Turanian languages allow of no grammatical petrifactions like those on which the relationship of the Aryan and Semitic families is chiefly founded. If they did they would cease to be what they are; they would be inflectional, not agglutinative. If languages were all of one and the same texture, they might be unravelled, no doubt, with the same tools."†

The greatest peculiarity of the languages and dialects about to be mentioned is their mutability.

---

* "Journ. Asiat. Soc. Bengal," 1875, vol. xliv. p. 308.
† "Science of Language," vol. ii. p. 25.

We are told of offshoot villages from a clan being formed across two or three mountain ranges distant from the parent valley, and in three generations the language of their grandfathers has become unintelligible to the colonists. Among civilized tribes, before we assumed any connection in race on the mere evidence of affinities discovered in their languages, we should naturally seek to ascertain in the first place whether any historic connection or intercourse had ever existed between them, by which they might have mutually influenced each other's speech. But among these rude and savage tribes, to be separate is to be hostile; each village, or at least each clan, is too isolated, and too jealous of its neighbours, to *borrow* from them any appreciable portion of their language. Where, then, we find an unmistakable affinity of speech, we may safely suppose an affinity of race and a common origin. But when we find a number of tribes differing from each other in dialect, preserving amongst them a large number of words or roots, which we discover again among certain other tribes separated by a great distance, with whom they have had no intercourse for ages, and these words not common to all of them, but some here and some there, the evidence of their mutual relationship is rendered much stronger. Such is the case with the two groups of languages or dialects we shall now compare. The first consists of those of the hill tribes of Arracan, viz. the Khyen, the Kami, the Kumi, the Mru and the Sak. The second consists of those of the Garo, the Kachári, the various Nága tribes, the tribes of the Manipúr valley, the Abor and Mishmi of Assam, and the Singpho. The words are taken, for the sake of easy reference, entirely from Hunter's Dictionary and the Rev. N. Brown's Tables. It will be seen that the corresponding roots are not found in all the dialects alike, but some in one, some in another; and it is singular that a large number of them are found among the Mru and Sak tribes that have been long under Burmese influence, and are said to be of the "same lineage as the Burmese."* Only a sufficient number of words to serve as a fair example are quoted, and all words which are common to the Burmese and other Tibetan dialects are omitted. Such are boat, day, fire, fish, hog, moon, road, and many others which belong to the mother-language of all the Tibeto-Burman dialects.

The first three numerals are either peculiar to each dialect by itself, or are founded on Tibetan roots; then follow:—

	Arracan Hill Tribes.	Nága, &c.	Burmese.
Four	ma-li	me-li	lay
	ta-li	a-li	
	pa-lu	pha-li	
Five	pang-gná	pha-ngá	ngá
	ta-ngá	ba-ngá	
Six	ta-ru	ta-ruk	khyouk
Seven	tha-ni	the-ne	koh-hnit

* Mason.

	Arracan Hill Tribes.	Nága, &c.	Burmese.
Eight	sat	i-sat	shit
Nine	ta-ku	ta-ku	kó
Ten	si-su	si	tsé
Twenty	hún	khún	nhit-tsé
Arrow	to-li-malá	malá	hmyá
	li	lá	
Bird	ta-vá	vá	hnget
	ta-wu	wu	
Blood	a-thi	a-thi	thway
Cow	tha-muk	sa-muk	nwá
Ear	ka-nhan	kha-na	ná
	a-ka-na	akhana	
Earth	ka-laí	klai, thalai	myay
Elephant	ka-sai	kasai	tsin
Hand	kuth	kut-pak	let
Head	lú	lu	goung
orn	a-rung	a-reng, rung	gyo
	ta-ki	ta-ki	
Horse	sapu	sapuk	myin
Mother	anu, nu	an-nu, onu	amay
Night	ayán	ayan	nya
Star	kirek	merik	kyé
Tree	tsindung	sundong	apin
	thin	thing	
Village	nam, thing	nam, ting	yua
Water	túi	tü, tui	yay

We have thus a large number of common words in which the Arracan dialects agree closely with the various dialects spread over the country extending north and west to the Brahmapútra river, and in which they differ from the Burman. The extent of the coincidence is too great to be fortuitous, and the past history and social condition of these tribes forbid our ascribing it to mutual intercourse and influence, such as have caused the adoption of several Hindustan words for domestic objects, in some of the Brahmapútra dialects.

We have thus collected into one group, more or less closely allied, the Chepang and other "broken tribes" of west Nipál, the Arracan hill tribes, and those various races to the east and south of the Brahmapútra. The next step will be to show the connection between these last and the Burman. That they belong to the Tibeto-Burman stock is generally conceded, it will only therefore need to take a few examples from three representative dialects, the Mikir, the Kuki, and Nága:

	Burmese.	Mikir.	Kúki.	Nága.
Bitter	khá	aké-ho	akhai	kékhu
Blood	thway		thi	thé-za
Eye	myet(k)	mék	mit	mhi
Eyebrow	myet-kon	mékúm	kemit-kho	
Fire	mee	mé	mei	mí
Fish	ngá		ngá	ná
Fruit	a-thee	athé		
Great	kyee	ké-thé		ké-di
House	eim	hém	in	
Kill	that		that tan	
Listen	ná-toung		ngai-tan	
Little	ngé		a-néo	
Long	shay		a-shao	
Moon	la		lhá	
Nose	na-koung	no-kan	nakúi	
Rice	tsan	sang	chang-chang	
Road	lan		lampi	lamá
Sick	ná		ana	
Tail	a-myee	armé	amei	mi
Water	yay	lang	tui	dzu (Kachári di)

The word "water" is singular in having preserved in each dialect a separate root, all differing from the Burmese. Thus the Kuki has the *tui* of the Arracan hill tribes, from the Chinese *sui*; the Nága has *dzu,* derived, like the Tibetan and Serpa *chu,* from the Chinese *chui*; the Kachári preserves the *ti* root of the Karen dialects in the form of *di* (d=t); while the Mikir *lang* seems to be derived from the Newar *la,* or more probably is a form of an archaic root preserved in the Kusunda *tang.* Thus these kindred and neighbouring dialects possess in this word "water" distinctive roots belonging to four widely-sundered, separate branches of Turanian speech. This can hardly be chance; still less probable is it that each deliberately *borrowed* its peculiar term; we must believe that each dialect in its earliest growth adopted and kept one of the many synonymous roots of the common mother Turanian language.

The first five numerals are given below, and it may be noted that they afford an instance of what Max Müller and other philologists have remarked of the tendency of these savage dialects to find separate expressions for the first and often the second numeral, while deriving the others from common roots.

	Burmese.	Mikir.	Kúki.	Nága.
One	Ta, tit	Isi	Khat	A-khet
Two	Hnit	Hi-ni	Ni, nik	A-ne
Three	Thóng	Ké-thom	Thum	A-sam
Four	Lay	Phi-li	Ll, li	Pha-li
Five	Ngá	Pha-nga	Ra-nga	Pha-nga

It will be seen that there is less resemblance to the Burmese forms than to some in the Himalayan dialects, especially to the Magar numerals, "one," *kat*; "two," *nis*; "three," *song*; "four," *bu-li*;

"five," *ba-nga*. The country of the Nága tribes has been already described; the Kukis extend over the hilly tracts from the valley of the Koladan in Arracan, where they border on the Kumis, to northern Kachár, where they march with the Mikir tribe on the Kopilee river. This latter clan (the Mikir) occupy the hills of the Nowgong district east of the Brahmapútra river. They are the furthest removed of all these tribes from possible Burman influence, and still they exhibit the closest affinity in language to the Burmese. It must, however, be said that these tribes, having probably the same origin as those of the Arracan hills, seem to have formerly occupied the whole mountainous country around the head-waters of the Kyendwen river, until in comparatively recent times they were driven westward by the Singpho, Abor, and Khamti races.

We have hitherto dealt with the wilder tribes on the western side of Burma, but there remains one great and important race which extends itself along the whole northern frontier of Burma Proper from Yunnan, where it is designated "Kakhyen," into Assam, where the tribes style themselves "Singpho," that is, "men" *par excellence*. It has been alleged that they are allied to the Karen race, and this by so late a writer as Anderson in his "Mandalay to Momien," published in 1876, but except their state of savage rudeness, and certain customs that are common to almost all the primitive tribes of these regions, there is really nothing to warrant this idea. On the contrary, a comparison of their vocabularies shows that, outside the common Indo-Chinese roots, all their lingual affinities are with the Burmo-Nága languages. The following are instances:—

	Burmese.	Nága Dialects.	Singpho.	Karen.
One	ta, tit	ama	ai-má	hta, la
Two	hnit		nkhong	'kie, nie
Three	thóng	a-sam	ma-sum	theu
Four	lay	a-li, be-li	me-li	lwie, lie
Five	ngá	mánga	ma-nga	yai
Six	khrouk	ta-ruk kruk (Chepang)	kru	khu, khoo
Seven	khoo-hnit	nith, i-ngnit	si-nith	nwi, nwai
I	ngá	ngai	ngai	ya, yer
Thou	nang, nin	nang	nang, ni	nah, ner
He	thoo	mih, kho (Tibet)	khi	awai, ur
Air	lay	ma-bung	m'bung	kli, li
Bird	hnget	ta-wu (Kumi)	wu	to, tu
Blood	thway	ai-chui	sai	thwi
Bone	aro	rha, kereng (Garo)	nrang	khi, kwi
Cow	nwá	masu	kan-su	po, k'lau
Dog	khway	kui	gui	htwi
Fire	mee	van	wan	may, mi
Flower	pan	taben	siban	paw
Hair	san	kra (Murmi) skra (Tibet)	kara	kho-thoo
Hand	let	lappa (Bhutan)	lettá	tsu, su
Head	khoung	gu-bong	bong	hko
Hog	wak	vak, vah (Horpa)	wa	to, htu
Horse	mrang	se rang (Chepang)	ka-mrang	ka-thi, thi
Moon	la	yita, lita	sita	lah
Mother	amay	annu, nu (Khyen)	nu	mo
River	mrach	kharr	khá	klo
Road	lam	lam	lam	klay
Salt	tsa	hum, sum	jum	itha, htula
Sun	nay	san, sanh	jan	mu, muh

In these examples some of the Burmese words are written as spelt, and not as pronounced, to show the true root. There is surely enough to warrant our affiliating the Singpho to the Nâga, and not to the Karen race, until the latter theory is proved by some incontestable evidence.

The Singpho or Kakhyens now fringe the whole northern frontier of Burma, extending from the Chinese province of Yun-nan into the valley of Assam. Their irruption into Assam took place about 1783, and is a comparatively modern instance of the flux and reflux which characterized the early movements of all these races. Cut off for centuries from their Nâga brethren, who at one time joined them in the upper valley of the Khyen-dwen river, as their tribes increased in numbers, they have had no room to expand eastward, owing to the barrier opposed by Chinese civilization; the Burman power checked them on the south; and they have thus been forced to use the only outlet afforded them, and partly retrace westward the route of their original migrations.

CHAPTER VI.

THE TAI OR SHAN RACE.

THE Tai or Shan race, although forming the least important element in the varied population of British Burma, affords an interesting ethnological study. The singular restlessness of this race, together with their aptitude under certain circumstances to concrete and form solid nationalities, in some degree entitles them to the designation of the Arabs of the Further East.

The national appellation of Tai, as above, is that used by all the branches of the race except the Siamese, who aspirate the word, *'tai,* giving it the signification of "free." The Tai race, under several local tribal names, but always one and the same people, occupies a far wider range than any other in the Indo-Chinese peninsula. In Assam, known as Ahoms, along the borders of Burma and China, it is divided into numerous semi-independent clans bearing in Burmese the generic name of Shans. Stretching southward, the same race, under the name of Laos, occupies the country between the Salween and Mekong rivers, while still further south, the best known and most civilized branch of the race, the Siamese, has founded a powerful maritime kingdom.

The Tai tribes, both in physical characteristics and in language, exhibit singular affinities to the Chinese, and yet they have derived their religion and literature entirely from their Burman and Cambodian neighbours. The southern tribes appear to have had little intercourse with the Chinese since the fourth or fifth centuries of the Christian era, and if we wish to trace out any connection between the two races we must look to a period far anterior to that in which we find them occupying their present relative positions.

That the Tai race is entirely distinct from both the Tibeto-Burman and the Mon-Anam is not for a moment to be doubted, while there is much to induce a belief that closer investigation will lead to the classification of the Tai tribes in a family of which the Chinese will be the representative branch.

The traditions of the people supply few hints of their pre-historic wanderings. But a consideration of their own historical movements and those of their neighbours, together with the geographical position they occupy, leads us to believe that both the Tai and Karen races came by a different route from that taken by the Burman and Mon-Anam families. The Tibeto-Burman tribes, which now form the Burmese nation, arrived, according to their traditions, in their present seats, from the westward, about six centuries before the Christian era. In confirmation of this we find a chain of fragmentary cognate tribes reaching from the Gunduk river in the west of Nipál to the banks of the Iráwadí, the footprints, as it were, of the march of their race. The upper course of the Iráwadí was at this time occupied by kindred tribes, which coalesced with that branch which founded the Burman monarchy and nation, but we find no mention of any precursors of alien origin.

At the same time we know that the south-eastern provinces of China, south of the Kin-sha-kiang, were occupied by the Tai race. Had their line of march been the same as that of the Burmans afterwards, we can hardly imagine that the nation would have forsaken the fertile valley of the Iráwadi to migrate, of their own accord, into the comparatively sterile hills of Yun-nan. All the probabilities are the other way;—that the Tai and other kindred tribes which the Chinese encountered, as the latter pressed southward into the great southern bend of the Kin-sha river, had followed the same route as the Chinese themselves, through Turkestan, and possibly striking the head-waters of the Kinsha, had pursued the course of that great river as it led them to the south.

Garnier (I. 466) says: "The 'Thai' race is among the last comers into Indo-China. An attentive comparison of Chinese history, the chronicles of Tonquin, and the traditions of the Tai themselves, induces the belief that anciently they formed part of the tribes called by the Chinese Pe-youe, who occupied until the commencement of our era all that part of China situated to the south of the Yang-tse-kiang."

"In the year 130 B.C., the Emperor Hiao-wou-ti achieved the conquest of the country of the Ye-lang and Ye-yu, comprising the north and east of Yun-nan, and the west part of Kwei-chow. The south-west angle of the province of Yun-nan was occupied by the principality of Tien, which extended to the city of Nanning, almost to the borders of the lake of Yun-nan, and was itself tributary to a great kingdom called Ma-mo. In the same region was the kingdom of Lao-Chin. We must doubtless look on these countries of Tien and Lao-Chin as Laotian principalities founded by emigrants of the Pe-youe tribes." (P. 470.)

All the traditions of the Tai tribes point to their gradual descent from the north through the valleys between the Salween and Mekong rivers. The formation of the various principalities of the Tai race in this region seems to have taken place in the period between the third century of our era and the fall of the Thang dynasty in China. We have seen that the Chinese empire was gradually, during this period, extending itself south of the Kinsha or Yang-tse-kiang, thus forcing the original inhabitants still further south. The earliest of these traditions is as follows.

Formerly, the countries now called Kiang Tung, Kiang Hung, and Muang Lem formed a vast plain, in the centre of which was a lake. The country was occupied by savages of the Khá race, who had formed seven kingdoms round the lake. The Tai principalities were Kiang Tung, Kiang Hung, Muang Lem, Kiang Tsen, which were subject to the Khás. The Prince of Kiang Hung had four sons. One day he addressed them thus: "The Khás are our masters. Let us shake off this shameful yoke and gain our independence."

His second son, Sonanta Kouman, entered the service of the Khá king, with a number of his countrymen. By his skill and bravery he became the favourite of the king, and after he had gained the latter's entire confidence, he treacherously murdered him with his principal chiefs, and made himself master of the whole country.

The earliest date in the Tai annals that we can accept with any degree of confidence is that of the foundation of Labong, in A.D. 574. The legend is of course embellished with the fabulous details usual in the native annals. It is remarkable that this date almost exactly corresponds with that of the Mon city and kingdom of Pegu. These various petty states occupying the region between the Salween and Mekong rivers, and on the east of the latter to the borders of Anam, are better known as the Laos States, aud form one of the great modern divisions of the Tai race, which are the Ahoms, Khamtis, Shans, Laos, and Siamese.

This was the name under which we find them in all the travellers of the sixteenth and seventeenth centuries.

> "Os Laos em terra e numero potentes
> Avàs, Bramas, por serras tam compridas."
> Lusiad, x. 126.

> "The Laos strong in number and in lands,
> Avàs and Bramas on their hills confined."

The modern Siamese recognize the Laos tribes as the stock from which they themselves sprung. They designate them the Thai-niai or Great Tai, and themselves the Thai-noi or Little Tai.

According to the Chinese historians, the western part of the province of Yun-nan formed, in the seventh century, a powerful Tai kingdom called Nan-tchao. About this time the Tai race spread over the region south of the Kinsha river to about lat. 18° N., where they bordered on the Cambodians, and eastward from the Iráwadí to the Mekong.

In the Burmese chronicles, mention is made of the destruction of the ancient city of Tagoung before the Christian era, and again of an invasion between A.D. 166–241, by a nation whom they style *Tarôk.* This term in modern Burmese is applied only to the Chinese; and hence English writers, not excepting even Sir A. Phayre, have heedlessly termed these early invaders Chinese. But the Tsin or Chinese Empire was, at the beginning of the Christian era, engaged in a struggle for national existence with the Turkish hordes, and did not for centuries afterwards approach its present south-western boundaries. If we assume the name *Tarók* to be identical with Turk, then these invaders could not possibly be Chinese. They were most probably tribes of the Tai race, seeking new seats for their increasing swarms. Whence the Burmese term *Tarók* arose it would be hard to say. We may offer the conjecture that at a later period in their history, when the Mongol armies of Kublai Khan again invaded Burma from the same direction as the earlier hordes, the Burmese historians confounded two different races, and gave both the name *Tarók*, which properly belonged to the Mongols, with whom they then became acquainted. According to the Assamese native chronicles a branch of the Tai race made their way into the valley of the Brahmaputra, about A.D. 780, and gradually made themselves masters of the whole of Assam. But they seem to have first formed a consolidated government, about A.D. 1228, under Chukupha, who assumed for his people the name of Ahoms or "peerless," by which name this branch of the Tai race was ever after distinguished from the others.

Towards the end of the thirteenth century the vast power and wide-reaching conquests of Kublai Khan, the great emperor of China, effected important changes in the condition of the Indo-Chinese peninsula. His conquest of Yun-nan drove out a large portion of the Tai race to seek new homes. His destruction of the ancient Burmese monarchy of Tagoung enabled those tribes of Tais, now known as Shans, to establish themselves as the masters of the upper valley of the Iráwadí, and, for a time, of the Burman kingdom itself. Fresh swarms pressed down on their brethren who occupied the upper valleys of the Salween and Mekong rivers. In A.D. 1293, a colony from the parent city of Labong founded the town of Xieng Mai, or, as it is called by the Burmese, Zimmay. Half a century later, one of the many petty kings of the Tai race on the western branch of the Menam, Phra Rama by name, advanced still further south and founded the city of Ayuthia on the site of the old Cambodian city of Lawek or Lovee. During the whole of this time the Tai race had evidently been pressing hard on the once famous and powerful empire of Cambodia. According to the account given by the King of Siam to Sir J. Bowring, "Our ancient capital of Ayuthia, before the year A.D. 1350, was but the ruin of an ancient place belonging to Kambuja (now known as Cambodia), formerly called Lawék, whose inhabitants then possessed southern Siam or western Kambuja. There were other cities not far remote, also possessed by the Kambujans. Some time near the year A.D. 1300, the former inhabitants were much diminished by frequent wars with the northern Siamese and the Peguans or Mons." From the founding of Ayuthia dates the formation of the nation and kingdom of Siam, which gradually extended itself until it reached the shores of the present Gulf of Siam, and thus divided the two great branches of the Mon-Anam race.

This division of the Tai race, now known to us as the Siamese, altered their national designation by aspirating the first letter, making it Htai, or Thai, as it is variously transliterated, with the signification of "free." They however recognized the fact that they were only an offshoot of the parent stock by styling the Laotian tribes the Tai-niai, or Great Tai, and themselves the Tai-noi, or Little Tai.

We have thus traced the emigration of the Tai race from their original seats on the south of the great Yang-tse-kiang river, and their establishment in an unbroken chain from the banks of the Brahmaputra to the waters of the Gulf of Siam. Nevertheless, superior as they are to the other races of the Indo-Chinese peninsula in numbers, in energy, and in physical characteristics, they are at this day everywhere, except in Siam, subject to some other power.

Still, as late as A.D. 1775, it appears that tribes of Tai race held an independent position, even in the country from which Chinese conquests had driven others of the same family. Garnier says: "The last struggle which the Chinese had to make in order to put down the unsubdued populations, who, under the names of Mau-tze and of Miao-tze, occupied certain mountain tracts of Kwei-chow and the banks of the

Kin-sha-kiang, only goes as far back as A.D. 1775. At that period the Miao-tze of the latter region were divided into two kingdoms, the Great Kin-tchouen and the Little Kin-tchouen. The capitals were called Lo-ou-ouei and Mamo. The Manchu general captured both these towns after a desperate resistance."

According to Edkins, "the Chung Miau (or Miao) are allied to the Siamese. They reside in the south-west of Kwei Chew province." "It appears from the vocabularies possessed by the Chinese of the Miau dialects that their tribes inhabiting the hill districts in Kweicheu, Kwangsi, and Yünnan are best regarded as a northern extension of the Siamese and Birmese population." The only error in this remark seems to be the reversing the position of the Siamese in the genealogical tree. These hill tribes, or at least some of them, are doubtless the representatives of the parent Tai race, of which the Siamese are a *southern* extension.

Garnier writes: "At the junction of the Kin-sha-kiang and Pe-chouy rivers we meet again with a Laotian population bearing there, as in the south, the name of Pa-y. This branch of the Tai race appears to have received its letters and civilization from Tibet." "The name of Pa-pe is a Chinese ethnological designation applied to all the Tai found between Xieng-mai (Zimmay) and Muong La. The specimens of Pa-pe writing given by Père Amyot indicate that their civilization is derived from the kingdom of Vienchan and Cambodia. The Pa-y, on the contrary, although *speaking exactly the same language*, seem to have obtained their system of writing from the Tibetans."

We thus see that at the present day the great Tai race still occupies the neighbourhood of the Great River, on whose banks the Chinese found them established eight centuries before the Christian era.

The present position of the different outlying branches of this widely-spread family may now be briefly traced. We shall take them in regular order from their furthest western point in Assam. It has been already stated that about A.D. 1228 the Tai king or chief (Chukupha, probably a corruption of the Tai title Choua-kooa-phra), having made himself master of Assam, changed the name of his people to Ahom, from whence the name Assam has been derived. His successor in A.D. 1554 became a convert to Hinduism, and from that period the Ahom Tai, gradually adopting the religion, the language, and the customs of the conquered people, have almost lost their nationality and become merged in the Hindu population.

Extending from Assam, along the northern frontiers of Independent Burma, the Khamti clans are the next representatives of the Tai family. They are Buddhists, and are described as possessing a fair degree of civilization. On the east they merge into the Shans.

The Shans are perhaps the most mixed of the Tai

race, at the same time that they have preserved most of their national characteristics. In the southern valleys of the hilly region between Bhamo and China we find them known as Shan-Tarôk, or Chinese Shans, a name expressive of their affinities. In the upper valleys of the Iráwadí and the Salween rivers they have been more or less affected by generations of intercourse with the Burmans, from whom they derived their religion and literature. This branch of the race is the most important as regards British Burma. Lying along the whole eastern frontier of Upper Burma, they are nominally subject to the Burman crown, but semi-independent, and only not wholly so from the want of cohesion among the petty states or clans into which they are split up. In the event of any future complications between the English and Burmese governments, they might form an important factor. A very little encouragement would induce all these clans to free themselves entirely from the feeble yoke of their Burman masters. A nation of traders, and delighting in a roving life, they would at once become our carriers into the western provinces of China, and open up that trade route which McLeod vainly attempted in 1836.

South of the Shan states, and occupying the wide region between the Salween river and the kingdom of Anam, lie the numerous tribes of Laos. Some of these are civilized, and have adopted both the Buddhist religion and letters, chiefly from the Burman source.

Others again are more or less savage, and, as remarked by Yule, may be regarded as the "deteriorated type of the progenitors of the Shans (the Tai) as they existed before the race was modified by Buddhist civilization." They are divided into two great divisions, the Black-bellies and the White-bellies, so termed as they do or do not adopt the practice of tattooing. The tattooed tribes occupy the districts of Zimmay, Labong, Lagon, and Muang Nan; the non-tattooers are found to the eastward of these in the districts of Muang Lom and Luang Phra-bang, and among the mountains separating Siam from Anam. The custom of tattooing is not one belonging to the Tai race, and is found only among those tribes which have been closely affected by Burmese influence, while the wilder and more distant tribes to the eastward, like the Siamese who have borrowed their customs from the old Cambodians, do not tattoo the body.

The country east of the Mekong river contains a medley of unclassified savage tribes, the broken and unpolished fragments of the various races that have occupied this portion of the peninsula. Garnier says: "The Does (Lawas) between Muong Yong and Xieng Tong call themselves Hoi-Mang. They say there are savages of the same origin as themselves, and speaking a similar dialect, dwelling on the banks of the Salween. They call these Hri-kun. I think we ought to affiliate to the Lawas, the Khas Mi, the Khmous and the

Lemet; all these tribes speak nearly the same language, and their customs offer great analogies." But this theory is not borne out by a comparison of these dialects as far as instances are supplied us by Garnier himself. The dialects of the Khmous and the Lemet certainly show more affinity to the Mon-Anam language than to the Tai or Shan. It is greatly to be regretted that the accomplished French explorers of this interesting region had not more acquaintance with the Mon-Anam languages, which would have helped to solve many points of difficulty. It can only be generally affirmed that the mountainous tract east of the Mekong river is the habitat of broken tribes of the Mon-Anam, the Tai, and perhaps the Tibeto-Burman, all more or less influenced by contact with more civilized and powerful neighbours.

South of the Laos states lies the kingdom of Siam, the most advanced and best known branch of the Tai family. Originally, as has been mentioned, a petty Laotian tribe, about the middle of the fourteenth century they founded the city of Ayuthia and the present Siamese monarchy. They gradually absorbed the best portion of the once great and flourishing empire of Cambodia, but they to a certain extent borrowed the civilization of the race which they supplanted. It is singular that at the two extremities of the wide area occupied by the Tai family, we find the only two cases of the people accreting into compact communities; and in both these cases the conquerors have yielded homage to the superior civilization of the conquered race by borrowing their religion and letters, and, in the case of the Ahoms, even their language.

PART II.

CHAPTER I.

Transliteration of Indo-Chinese Languages.

The transliteration of Eastern languages into the Roman character has engaged the attention of scholars, of missionaries, and latterly of Government. There is confessedly no perfect system, even in the opinion of those who advocate one or the other of those put forward. It would seem that Professor Max Müller looks on the general adoption of any one system as hopeless.

But in the languages of the Indo-Chinese peninsula the attempt to render the written and the spoken word by the same set of Roman characters is simply impossible. In these languages the different modifications of the vowel sounds by various final consonants, or, as in Mon and Cambodian, by the initial consonant as it is a surd or a sonant, can never be represented by any arbitrary system. In the "Journal of the Royal Asiatic Society," 1878, Mr. St. Barbe showed, with respect to Burmese, that the only safe or useful method is to give up all idea of representing at the same time the written and the spoken word, except by two sets of characters. While not quite agreeing with all the details of his system, it is, I believe, founded on the only right principle.

For purely scientific and philological purposes the word should be given in the consonant and vowel symbols corresponding to those of which it is actually composed. The sound is often a mere accidental or local peculiarity. Of course in unwritten languages we can simply write the sounds as nearly as possible in Roman letters. For the purposes of comparison between different dialects, a knowledge of the variation between the spoken and the written language is necessary. To give an instance. We are at once enabled to connect together the Abor *a'lak*, the Singpho *letta*, the Burmese *lak*, "hand," because we know that, though the Burmese written form is as above, the spoken form is *let*.

For all ordinary purposes, and for works intended for popular use, the sound alone should be considered, and truly represented; while in those chiefly intended for scholars the double form, both as written an spoken, should be given. In the former case it is easy, with regard to important proper names, to add also the proper spelling.

CHAPTER II.

ALPHABETS.—All derived from Pali of second to fifth century.—Reasons.—Burmese from Mon.—Anamese adopted Chinese system.—Peculiar system of Mon and Cambodian.—Siamese alphabet from Cambodian.—Shan or Laos from Burmese.—Number of vowel sounds.—Why necessary in monosyllabic languages.—Tones.—Mon and Cambodian not tonal.—Tones in Siamese, Shan and Ahom.

THE various alphabets in use among the nations of the Indo-Chinese countries have all been primarily derived from that form of the ancient Pali character which prevailed in India about the fourth or fifth century after Christ. The introduction of Buddhism, and with it letters and books, into the two earliest civilized states on the eastern side of the Bay of Bengal, is ascribed to the famous teacher Buddhaghosa. This man was a Brahmin of Magadha, who, after visiting Ceylon, about A.D. 400, to make a recension of the sacred Buddhist writings, became the apostle of Buddhism and civilization in the countries east of the Bay of Bengal. At that period the seaboard along the Gulf of Martaban, the Gulf of Siam, and the shores of the China Sea, were inhabited by the Mon-Anam race, the Mons of Pegu, the Khmers of Cambodia, and the Anamese on the east.

From the Mons and Khmers, the inland tribes, the Burmans, Siamese, Laos, and Khamti derived more or less directly their respective alphabets. The Anamese came so early and so closely under Chinese influence that it is doubtful whether they ever possessed a character derived from India. There are no traces of it, and they have from the earliest recorded times used an adaptation of the Chinese phonetic characters.

If the different alphabets in use among the Indo-Chinese nations are examined it will be easily seen that they can be divided into two classes, as they are derived from the Mon or the Cambodian (Khmer) types. Thus the modern Siamese and the Shan *k* are formed from the element of a single incomplete circle like the Cambodian, whilst the Burmese, the Laos, and the Khamti *k* consist, like the Mon, of two incomplete circles joined.

Although both the Mon and Cambodian alphabets plainly owe their existence to a Pali source, they differ in many respects both from each other and from the parent character. Each has retained certain of the ancient forms which the other has rejected, and each approaches nearer in some forms to the Indian rock-cut inscriptions than does the other.

Thus the Mon retains the circle with a dot ⊙, the *th* of the Pali inscriptions, though giving it the power of *b*, which does not exist in the Cambodian. This latter again has preserved the ancient form of *t* which is quite changed in the Mon. The Cambodian writing is much more cursive than the Mon, and it is not an improbable surmise that this is due to the higher degree of civilization and literary excellence to which the former nation attained, and which led to a considerable modification of the original stiff and cramped forms of the letters.

Both history, and natural presumptions lead to the belief that the other alphabets now existing in the Indo-Chinese peninsula are, as before said, derived originally from the Cambodian or Mon types. But they also contain internal evidence to the same effect.

Both the Mon and Cambodian have followed the Pali-Sanskrit system of arranging and classifying the consonants in *vargas* or rows, retaining in their places all the different symbols, although altering their powers, and have likewise preserved two characters which complete the Indian alphabet. These are the *anusvára* (°), which serves in Mon both as a vowel symbol, *au* or *o*, and also as a nasal final, and the *visarga* (꞉) or weak final *ă*. The Burmese employs this last as a symbol of tone, and makes no use of the cerebrals in writing pure Burman words, while the Shan and the Khamti have entirely omitted them from their system. It is clear that the alphabets which contain the Pali-Sanskrit elements most completely are the nearest to the fountain head, and could not have been derived from the more imperfect forms.

There is a resemblance so striking in one peculiarity of the Mon and Cambodian writing that this in itself goes far to show the intimate connection between the languages. It is the division of the consonants into the surds and sonants with a different effect on the inherent vowel. In the Cambodian this is the more pronounced and uniform; every sonant has an inherent *o* involved in its formation, instead of the inherent vowel *a* belonging to the surds in this, and common to both surds and sonants in Burmese, Shan, Tibetan and kindred languages. In Mon the same division of the consonants is made, and when a sonant is followed by a final consonant without a vowel symbol the inherent vowel has the sound of *ō*. When a sonant stands alone the inherent vowel has a sound nearly resembling the French *éa*, the two syllables pronounced shortly together and yet distinct. The Siamese, which has undoubtedly borrowed its system of writing from the Cambodian, adopts *ō* as the inherent vowel throughout the alphabet.

PART III.

COMPARATIVE GRAMMAR OF THE MON-ANAM FAMILY.

SECTION I.

VOWELS.—Table of vowels.—*a* and *á*, *i* and *í*, *u* and *ú*, *e* and *ê*, *o*.—Mon diphthongs.—The Pali *anusvâra* and *visarga*. CONSONANTS.—The whole Pali system adopted.—Additional characters.—Table of consonants.—Permutation of surds and sonants.—Gutturals. — Palatals. — Dentals. — Labials. — Semi-vowels. — Initial and final consonants.—Double consonants. ROOTS.—Monosyllabic, how explained.—Anamese tones.—Double consonants in Mon and Cambodian.—Compound roots.

Ă and *ā*.—Mon and Cambodian have each two sounds, the short sound of the inherent vowel, as in "salute," and the long sound, which is really composed of two *a*'s *aa*, as in father. The Anamese has a second short sound, differing little from the sound of the inherent vowel.

In Mon the *ā* followed by *k* or *ng* becomes modified into *ai*, the Greek sound *εἶ*. The short vowel *ă*, which is not expressed in writing, is in like manner modified by a following consonant. With *k* and *ng* it takes the sound of long *ā*, and with all the others that of *au* in "caught."

As before observed, preceding consonants of the sonant class also modify the sound of the inherent *ă*, in the Cambodian universally into *o*, but in Mon, when without a final consonant, into a sound like the French *éa*, and when followed by a final consonant into *o*, except in the case of *k* and *ng* when the sound is that of broad *a* (*ā*). The long *ā* in Mon is modified by a preceding sonant into a sound similar to the *a* in the same circumstances, but more pronounced. In Cambodian after the sonants *ā* becomes *éa*. This peculiar system of modification is unknown to the Tibetan, Burmese, and Karen languages. In the Anamese there are slight traces of it, but it would be almost impossible to ascertain the original laws of sound in the Anamese under its Chinese system of phonetics and intonations.

I, ī and *u, ū*.—The short *i* in Mon has before a final *k* and *ng* a sound between long and short *ei*. The *u* resembles the Italian *u* or French *ou*. The long *ī* and *ū* call for no remarks. In Cambodian the sounds are modified as they follow surds or sonants. After the former *i* and *ī* become *ĕ* and *ĕy*, *u* and *ū* become *o* and *au*. After the sonants the sounds are the same as in the Mon.

E, ē.—In both Mon and Cambodian the sound is that of the French *é* or the English *ay* as in "day," except that in Mon before final *k* and *ng* it sometimes has the sound of *ei*.

O, ó is very largely used in both Cambodian and Anamese, but does not exist as a simple vowel in Mon. In Cambodian the short *o* forms the inherent vowel of all consonants of the sonant class, and also takes the place of the *u* sound after the surds. In Mon the *anusvára* supplies the want, and before a final gives the sound of short *ŏ* after a surd and of long *ō* after a sonant. But this vowel is itself really only a compression of *au*; so we find that in Mon *au* has the sound of *ow* as in "cow," or when followed by a final the sound of *ō*.

The *visarga*, or final weak *h*, is found in both the Mon and Cambodian with the same power, giving a sharp quick sound to the final vowel. In the Cambodian, it is in most cases (says Aymonier) indifferent whether this sound is represented in writing by this symbol or by a final *s*.

The Mon, Cambodian and Anamese languages are rich in compound vowel sounds, which have no place in Pali. The two former have therefore been obliged to invent new symbols, or make modifications of the existing, to represent these various shades of sound. The Mon is singular in having certain triphthongs, or combinations of three vowel symbols.

Oä, as in "boar," seems confined to the Mon. This symbol and *ā* are combined as a diphthong and have the sound of *ai* in "aisle." Combined with *u* it has the sound of *ué* or *oo-ay*. The combination of the symbols for *i*, *u*, and *oă* has the same sound. The symbol of *oă* combined with that of *é* represents the sound *é-ow*. Finally the symbols of *é*, *oă*, and *á* combined form a sound *oă* similar to the simple *oă*. This vowel symbol does not exist in the Cambodian writing nor in the derived Siamese. But it is found in the Burmese in the second form mentioned above representing the sound *ai* in "fair."

Au, ow (Greek *ου*).—These sounds are represented in Mon and Cambodian by the combined symbols *é* and *ā*, which form the Pali *ō*. In Mon, when this diphthong is followed by a final consonant, it always has the sound of *ō*. In Cambodian it has the sound of *ō* when following a surd, and of *ow* when coming after a sonant. The long form of the diphthong does not exist in Pali. In Mon, a dash over the consonant to the right has been adopted to represent it, with the sound of *ow*. In Cambodian the dash is not used alone, but is placed above the combination of the symbols *é* and *ā* as above, and the whole takes the sound of *au* after a surd and of *ou* as in French after a sonant.

Ai.—In Mon, this sound is formed by the combination of the symbols *i* and *u* before *k* and *ng*. Before all other finals, after a surd, the diphthong has the sound of broad *ā*, but after a sonant nearly the sound of the short *u* in "pull." This combination of *i* and *u* is wanting in Cambodian.

U'o'.—The Cambodian and the Anamese both possess this peculiar vowel sound, which is difficult to represent truly in Roman characters, and is the combination of the symbols *o'* and *i*. There is also in Cambodian a simple sound of *uo* which is merely the combination of the symbols *uu*.

The Cambodian possesses several distinguishing symbols for various slightly differing sounds of the *é*, which do not exist in the Mon. These are simply modifications of the original Pali symbol of the simple *é*.

Consonants.

The Mon and the Cambodian divide the consonants into *vargas* or rows like the Pali. But besides the thirty-three symbols, including the *aṇusvâra* of the Pali, the Mon and the Cambodian have each two additional characters.

Gutturals	*k*	*kh*	*k*	*kh*	*ng*
Palatals	*ch*	*chh*	*ch*	*chh*	*ny*
Cerebrals	*t, d*	*th*	*d, t*	*th*	*n*
Dentals	*t*	*th*	*d, t*	*th*	*n*
Labials	*p, b*	*ph*	*p*	*ph*	*m*
Semi-vowels	*y*	*r*	*l*	*v, w*	
Sibil. and Aspir.	*s*	*h*	*l*	*h* (final)	
Additional: Mon			*b*	*bh*	
Additional: Cambodian			*s*	*ṣ*	

In the above table, where two powers are given for

the same letter as *t, d,* the first is Mon, the second Cambodian.

Gutturals.—The Mon and Cambodian, although adopting all the Pali characters, and using the series of surds and sonants to modify the succeeding vowel sound, have only one guttural, *k,* and its aspirate *kh.* The sound of *g,* the sonant, is not found in Cambodian, and only exists in Mon in words beginning with the nasal *ng,* where the *g* is sounded initially, as *now,* pronounced *gnow.* The Anamese preserves the *g* and its aspirate fully.

Palatals.—The Cambodian only possesses the palatal sound *ch,* and its aspirate *chh.* In Mon we find these Pali characters are used to represent not only the palatal *ch,* but also the sounds *s, ts, z*; but it is most probable that these are later corruptions, and that the original sound was *ch* and a variation like a *very* soft *sh.**

Cerebrals.—Although the Mon and Cambodian, like many other of the Ultra-Indian alphabets, have adopted the whole of the characters in this *varga* from the Pali in order to complete the system, they make little use of them. They prefer the corresponding dentals. The Burmese indeed make no use of them at all in purely native words. The Shan alphabets again reject them altogether. In Mon the characters representing the

---

* Max Müller says *ch* may be said to consist of half *t* and half *sh.*

sonants *ḍ* and *ṇ* are used as initials, the latter only in a few words. The Cambodian reverses the powers of the Pali charactérs, and thus represents the surd *ṭ* by the character of the sonant *ḍ*, and *vice versâ*. The aspirates are very seldom used. The *ṇ* is used but rarely.

Dentals.—The character represented as *th* is an aspirated *t*, not the sound of *th* in "thin," "that," which is not found in Mon, Cambodian or Anamese, although common in the Tibeto-Burman languages. In Cambodian only the dental surds, as represented by the Pali characters, and the nasal, are used. The sonant *d* is sufficiently, it seems, supplied by the *ḍ* in the cerebral *varga*. In Mon the characters of the Pali sonants are often pronounced as surds. In Anamese *d* has often a sound as if followed by a liquid *i*, thus *dam* is pronounced *diam*.

Labials.—In Mon the sonant Pali letters of the labial *varga*, although retained, are oftener given the sound of *p* than of *b*. The true labial sonant and its aspirate *bh* are supplied by two extra characters not contained in the Pali or Sanskrit alphabets. In Cambodian the same transformation happens in this as in the cerebral *varga*; the Pali letters representing the surd *p* and the sonant *b* have their powers reversed. But in both these cases, when the Pali symbols stand before another consonant they resume their original sounds of *t* and *p*. The aspirate *ph*, in both Mon and

Cambodian, is a simple aspirated *p*, and never has a sound approaching *f*. The Anamese, on the contrary, gives to *ph* the sound of *f*, which is evidently the result of Chinese influence. *M* final in Mon and Cambodian always preserves its proper sound, and may be written interchangeably with the *anusvâra*, never taking a nasal sound as in Burmese.

Semi-vowels.—Mon has *y*, *r*, *l*, *w*, and also the Pali *ḷ*, but this last is little used. The Cambodian has *y*, *r*, *l*, *v*, and also *ḷ*, merely to complete the series of letters corresponding to the Pali *varga*. The Anamese has only *r*, *l*, *v*. The Mon *w*, when final after any vowel, and the Cambodian *v*, after *au*, *u*, *ū̄*, *ou*, in no way affect the sound of the preceding vowel; thus, *kow* is pronounced *ko*, *kéw* as *ké*. In Mon, when a consonant without a vowel is followed by *w*, the inherent vowel has the sound of *aw*.

Sibilants and Aspirate.—Mon has one *s*, the same character as in Pali, which the Burmese turns into *th*. The Cambodian has two additional characters with the same power as the common *s*. The Anamese has no true sibilant, but possesses a sound of *sh*, occurring at the commencement of words. The aspirate is common to all three languages.

The character of the primitive or inherent *a* is also used in Mon and Cambodian as a final consonant. The Mon has two characters peculiar to itself in addition to the labial sonants borrowed from the Pali, *b*, *bh*, which are in more frequent use than the Pali *b*. The Anamese has a peculiar guttural, which the French transliterate by *x* with the sound of *cs*.

Roots.

The languages of the Mon-Anam family are classed among those styled *monosyllabic* or *isolating*. Of this class of languages the Chinese is the most perfect example. It must, however, be remembered that the term monosyllabic does not actually mean that every word consists of only one syllable. There are many dissyllabic words, especially in the Mon and Cambodian. But each of these syllables is a distinct and separate root word, with a meaning of its own. To use the expression now generally made use of in philological treatises, if the sign R be taken to stand for the simple primitive root, then such words are composed of $R+R$. The various relations of time and place are expressed by an independent root prefixed or suffixed to the principal root, and no change whatever takes place in the roots themselves.

The simple root is detached from all idea of relation, and "may be employed to convey the meaning of great, greatness, greatly, and to be great,"—that is, the abstract idea only, the accidents of relation to other things being shown either by position in the sentence or by the addition of other roots.

The monosyllabic languages have only a limited

number of radical syllables; the Chinese has about five hundred. In order to make this number serve to express a greater number of ideas, and at the same time to preserve a distinction between these homonyms, several of the languages which have come under Chinese influence have adopted the system of tones. Of the Mon-Anam family, only the Anamese has done this. The Cambodian and Mon are both spoken *recto tono*. Among the remaining languages of Ultra-India, the Siamese, Shan, and Karen are all acknowledged to have adopted the tonal system. The Tibetan and Burman are generally represented as without these tones, but there is no doubt that this is incorrect. The Burman language possesses three tones, although Judson and others have termed the signs used to distinguish them "accents." Dr. Jaeschke affirms that the tonal system is gradually taking possession of the Tibetan language, in consequence apparently of the loss, in colloquial pronunciation, of the double initial consonant which occurs in so many words in the written language. This, as Dr. Edkins observes, goes to show that the tones are merely an adventitious help towards distinguishing homonyms. The same theory is further established by the comparison of the languages of the Mon-Anam family. The Cambodian and Mon abound in words with double initial consonants like the Tibetan,* but in the Anamese the same roots are found

* Consisting of *t* and *k* prefixed to the consonants *ng*, *d*, *n*, *m*, *r*, *l*, *w*, *b*.

deprived of the first initial consonant. Thus, Mon *t'gnoa,* Cambodian *thgnay,* "day," is in Anamese *gnay.* Mon *k'sim,* "bird," becomes in Anamese *chim; b'mok,* "east," becomes *moc.* It is evident that either the Anamese has at some time lost the extra initial consonant, or that the Mon and Cambodian have at some time made an addition to the primitive root, to satisfy the need for distinction between homonymous words. Many of the dissyllables in Mon are nouns formed from simple verbal roots by the addition of the initials *t* or *k*; but a permutation often takes place when the initial of the primitive root is one that does not enter into the series of compound consonants. Thus, from *kloo,* "dark," by the addition of *t* initial and the permutation of *m* for *k,* is formed *t'mloo,* "darkness"; from *klaut,* "to steal," is formed, in a similar manner, *k'mlaut,* "a thief."

Other dissylables are formed by the juxtaposition of two roots, *R + R;* thus, *p'kaw,* "to break," is formed of the roots *pa,* "to do," and *kaw,* "to break."

SECTION II.

NOUNS.—Verbal roots formed by combination *R* + *R*.—Cambodian simple roots. GENDER.—Only as regards animate beings.—Special signs. NUMBER.—Mode of distinguishing it.—Common to all languages of this class.—Burmese.—Chinese. CASE.—None. —Relations of things, how expressed. ADJECTIVES.—Verbal noun.—Formed by addition of verb "to be."—Participial adjectives largely used in all languages of High Asia.—Comparison, how expressed. NUMERALS.—Importance of numerals in comparison of languages.—Paradigm of Mon-Anam numerals.—Important deductions therefrom. PRONOUNS.—Table of Mon-Anam pronouns.—Substitutes for personal pronouns.—Relative pronouns.—Demonstrative.—Interrogative.—Honorific. VERBS.—The verb either a single root, or *R* + *R*.—No change to express mood or tense.—Accidents, how distinguished.—Present. —Past.—Future.—Imperative.—Passive voice, none.—Passivity, how expressed.—Negative.—Construction of sentence.—Verbal root with complement of time &c. used as subject.—Paradigm of verb. ADVERBS. PREPOSITIONS. CONJUNCTIONS. PARTICLES.

THERE are in the Mon-Anam languages two kinds of nouns, simple and compound. The first class consists of primitive roots; as, Mon *kon*, "son," Cambodian *se*, "horse," Anamese *cay*, "tree." The second class includes nouns formed in various ways from verbal roots.

Of the latter some consist merely of two roots, which remain distinct and unaffected in form, except by euphonic permutation. This being the case, it seems difficult to refer these languages strictly to the *isolating* class, as is generally done. Take, for example, Mon *tataumeh-chyăt,* "death"; here the two roots, *tataumeh,* "to be," and *khyăt,* "to die," are simply placed in juxtaposition to form the abstract noun "death." In Anamese, "goodness," *su'lành,* is formed from *lành,* "good," and *su',* "thing." What is this but agglutination?

Other nouns are formed from single verbal roots. Mon is especially rich in these, and forms them in a variety of ways, by changing or modifying the initial consonant. Thus, *katow,* "hot, to be hot," *k'mtow,* "heat"; *kasăt,* "to kill," *k'msăt,* "death"; *klaut,* "to steal," *k'mlaut,* "a thief." Also by prefixes, as from *yĕh,* "to shine," *layĕh,* "light"; from *pnīk,* "to trade," *păpnīk,* "merchandise"; *hăm,* "to speak," *lăhăm,* "speech"; *pyoo,* "to make a noise," *t'myoo,* "a sound. This facility of forming nouns is not equally shared by the Cambodian and Anamese. In the former, most nouns are simple roots; while in the latter, although nouns are formed from verbal roots by the use of the prefix *su',* "thing," as mentioned above, yet this is not general, and is opposed to the genius of the language.*

---

* Aubaret, "Gram."

Other substantives in Anamese are formed by the union of two roots with approximate meanings: thus *nin,* "to be silent, and *lăng,* "to be calm," joined together express "silence." In this Anamese resembles Chinese, which, in like manner, forms many words by the juxtaposition of two roots of similar signification; thus, *kenyouen* (root-origin) conveys the meaning of "beginning." Both the Tai and Karen languages possess a like power of forming compound nouns.

In Anamese we also find great use made of certain distinguishing prefixes. Thus the word *con,* "son," enters into combination with a great number of simple roots of various classes to form the perfect noun; as *con cho,* "a dog," *con trai,* "a son," *con cá,* "a fish," *con mát,* "the eye," *condâu,* "a seal." The word *cây,* "a tree," is prefixed to the names of particular trees, as *cây cau,* "betel-nut tree," *cây mit,* "jack-tree." There are several other of these prefixes, for fruits, vegetables, and objects of different kinds. The same system, but to a less extent, may be observed in the Mon; thus, *tnom,* "a tree," is prefixed to the specific names of trees, as *tnom krout,* "mango tree," *tnom tó,* "cotton tree." To the names of various kinds of fish the word *ká,* "a fish," is prefixed, as *ká wöa,* "a shark," *ká pān,* "an eel." In Burmese, as well as Chinese and other East Asian languages, similar compounds are found; but in these the appellative is, with few exceptions, a suffix and not a prefix of the radical noun.

These appellatives must not be confused with the numerical affixes which are found in the Chinese, Tibeto-Burman, Malay, Polynesian, and Mexican languages. The Cambodian does not seem to use them, but they exist in the dialect of the wild Stiens, in the highlands of the Mekong valley, which has preserved many archaic forms of the Mon-Anam language, that have ceased to be common to the civilized branches of the family. The Cambodian is, moreover, far simpler in its radical forms than the Mon.

Gender.—In the Mon-Anam, as in all the languages of the Turanian family, distinction of gender is only applied to things endowed with animate life. Even of these, a few only, in what may be termed the highest scale of existence, are deemed to belong inherently to either gender. Such are man, woman, husband, wife, father, mother. Caldwell says: "The unimaginative Scythians reduced all things, whether rational or irrational, animate or inanimate, to the same dead level, and regarded them all as impersonal. They prefixed to common nouns, wherever they found it necessary, some word denoting sex, equivalent to male or female, he or she; but they invariably regarded such nouns as in themselves neuter, and generally they supplied them with neuter pronouns."

Even for terms so "instinct with personality" as man and woman, the Mon has no distinctive terms, but uses a sexual affix, as *mneh*, "man," *mneh prayër*, "woman."

These sexual affixes are in Mon *trong*, masculine, *prayër*, feminine, for human beings; as *kon trong*, "a boy, or son," *kon prayër*, "a daughter:" for animals, *k'mat* and *bŭh*; as *klaër k'mat*, "a bullock," *klaër bŭh*, "a cow." In Cambodian the gender of names of human beings is expressed in the same way by *pros*, masculine, and *srey*, feminine; that of animals by *chhmoul*, masculine, and *'nhi*, feminine. The Anamese masculine affix for names of rational beings, is *trai*, and the feminine *gai*; as *con trai*, "a boy," *con gai*, "a girl." With quadrupeds *du'c* indicates the male and *cái* the female, while with birds the affix *trong* is masculine and *mái* feminine; as *gà trong*, "a cock," *gà mái*, "a hen." In this manner of expressing gender the Mon-Anam dialects agree with all the Tibeto-Burman, Shan, and Karen languages.

Number.—In none of the Mon-Anam languages is the singular distinguished, except by using the numeral *one*, nor is the root in any way altered to express the plural. Thus in Mon, *mneh cheer* may in itself mean either "the man is eating," or "the men are eating." To denote a plural number definitely, the affix *taw* (literally "to increase") is used; as *mneh taw cheer*. The indefinite plural is sometimes represented by *k'mlung*, "many"; as *mneh k'mlung kong*, "men are coming."

In the same manner, in Cambodian, the plural is signified by the use of *cheron*, "many," and *âs*, "all," after the noun. But here exists also a curious mode of denoting a number by using two numbers nearly approximate to that which is intended. Thus, "I see horses" may be expressed by "I see two or three, four or ten horses," as the case may be.

In Anamese, which in this particular differs from its sister dialects, the plural is denoted by the particles *chung, cac, mây, nhữ'ng, phô*, prefixed to the noun. But to express "men" the particle *ta* is often used after the noun. This particle is the Chinese *ta*, "great," the sign of the plural, and is the Mon plural particle *taw*, "to increase."

In their manner of expressing the relations of gender and number the Mon-Anam languages agree with the general principle of all their neighbours. In the Tibeto-Burman dialects the plural particles follow the nouns, as in the Mon and Cambodian, while the Anamese has borrowed from the Chinese, and followed its idiom in prefixing the particle.

Numeral affixes, which are found in all the languages of Indo-China, and most of those allied to the Mongolian family, the Polynesian, and even the ancient Mexican, are made use of in the Mon and Anamese, but not in the Cambodian. The use of them is, however, limited, and the affixes may in many instances be dispensed with. Thus, it is quite correct to say in Mon, *m'nĕh paun,* "men four," or *t'row tnom,* "six trees," and in Anamese *bốn ngu'o'i,* "four men," but we *must* express this in Burmese by "men four beings" and "trees six plants."

Case.—In what is merely intended as a short synopsis of the relations between the different members of the Mon-Anam family, it will suffice to say that, in common with all others of the isolating languages, they possess no forms of declension or case. The accidents of time and place, and the reciprocal relations of nouns to each other, are expressed by means of location or the use of prepositions.

The genitive case is distinguished by placing the the thing possessed before the possessor, as in Mon *sgnee meh öa,* "house-father-I," or "my father's house." Other accidents of relation are represented by prepositions, as *padöa sgnee,* "in the house."

This inversion of the genitive and use of prefixes forms a clear line of division between what Logan calls the eastern and western Himalayan languages, among which latter are classed the Tibeto-Burman dialects. The Chinese seems to occupy a middle place between the two. It marks the genitive case, either by the use of a particle *tchi,* placed between the two nouns and answering to the Tibetan *gi,* or by the position, placing the word in the genitive first, as in the English "my father's house." In the locative case the Chinese can employ either a prefix or a suffix; in all the other cases prepositions are used.

Adjectives.—In the Mon-Anam languages, as in all those of cognate origin, there are no independent adjectives, as in the Indo-European family, agreeing with their qualified substantives in gender, number, and case. What we term adjectives are either (1) verbal roots, (2) simple nouns, (3) participles of verbs, used to qualify the noun to which they are attached. Thus, in "a good man," *good* is the simple verbal root; in "a gold cup," *gold* is a noun itself, used to qualify the noun accompanying it; and in "upright men," *upright* is expressed by "being true."

The adjective, or qualifying word, always follows the noun which it qualifies, as "man good." This post-position of the qualifying word is common to the Tibeto-Burman and all other languages of Indo-China, while the Chinese alone place the adjective before the noun.

The comparative degree is expressed by adding in Mon *lōn*, "very," in Cambodian *cheang* or *lœus*, "more," in Anamese *h'on*, "more," to the qualifying word. The superlative, in like manner, is expressed in Mon by *ōt*, which means "all," "ended," "exhausted," added to the adjectival noun. In Cambodian the words *nas*, *pek*, "very," placed at the end of the phrase, are used for the same purpose. In Anamese also the same word *rát*, "very," prefixed to the adjective, or the words *lām, qua,* "much," following it, are used to set forth the superlative degree.

Numerals.—Professor Max Müller, in his letter "On Turanian Languages," remarks on the importance of the numerals in a comparison of different dialects, and also notices that in allied savage languages we often find the first two numerals different, while the others show more or less signs of a common derivation.

In modern Cambodian the numeration is quinary, that is, six is five-one, seven is five-two, &c. Garnier, however, gives a regular series of ten distinct numerals in old Cambodian (ii. 506). But the quinary system was in vogue towards the end of the thirteenth century, according to the valuable account of the Chinese official whose narrative has been translated by A. Rémusat.

It has been already shown, in the remarks on the Mon-Anam family, how important is the evidence afforded by the numerals, of the connection between its several branches. We shall further find that the *ancient* forms of the Cambodian numerals are met with in savage dialects of the present day, which are thus shown to have preserved the original roots; unless indeed we adopt the scarcely credible hypothesis that the ancient, highly-civilized Cambodians borrowed their numerals from their wild, uncivilized neighbours. Again, we shall find a most distinct resemblance in the numeral roots between the language of the Mons of Pegu and that of the petty savage tribes on the banks of the far-distant Mekong river.

One.—The same root runs through all the various Mon-Anam dialects. The representation of the sounds of unwritten languages must, of course, depend on the fancy of the individual transcriber; still the root generally remains recognizable. Thus, we find the first numeral to be in Mon *mooă*, in old Cambodian *mouay*, in modern *muy*, in Anamese *mốt*, and in the savage dialects of the tribes of the valley of the Mekong, (the Samre) *moe*, (the Xong) *moi*, (the So) *mouei*, (the Khmous and Mi) *moui*, and (the Stieng) *mouoi*. Several other dialects, as given by Garnier, have the same forms as the above.

Two.—The Mon form of the second numeral, *bă*, is evidently the simple root. Garnier gives *bar* as the form in ancient Cambodian, in the Stieng, So, Mi, Khmous, Souc, and other dialects. The modern Cambodian is *pî*, which form is followed by the Samre *pea*. The Xong has *pra*, and the Anamese *hai*, both anomalous forms.

Three.—The third numeral in Mon is *pi* (*pee*). In old Cambodian this is *peh*, in modern *bè*, in Stieng *pey*, in Samre, Xong, Mi, Khmous *pe*, in So *pei*. The Anamese form *ba* is again anomalous.

Four.—The same root is common to all the dialects, with slight modifications. Mon has *paun* (*pōn*), old Cambodian *pon*, modern *buốn*, Samre, Xong *pon*, Stieng, Souc, So, Khmous, *pouốn*, Anamese *bốn*.

Five.—There are two distinct forms of this numeral.

Allied to the Mon *m'son* or *p'son* are the So, Souc, and Huei *soung*, and the Hin and Nanhang *choung*. The other root is *pram* of the Cambodian, both old and modern, found also in the Samre, the Xong, and the Stieng; and of this the Anamese *nam* is probably only another form.

Six.—The Mon, Cambodian, and Anamese all differ in the remaining numeral forms. The Mon six, *trow*, is found in the Souc *troou*, the Huei *treou*, and the Banar *totrou*. The Stieng *prao*, and perhaps even the old Cambodian form *krong*, may be referred to the same root. The modern Cambodian has *pram muy*=five-one. The Anamese *sau* stands alone.

Seven.—In the Mon form *t'pauh* (*t'poh*), the aspirated initial letter is not a part of the root, but belongs to the class of prefixed consonants common in Mon. The same remark applies to *m'song*, "five," *t'row*, "six," *t'sam*, "eight," *t'seet*, "nine." We find the Mon root in the Stieng *po*, the Banar *topo*, the Souc *pho*, and the Hin *thpol*. The old Cambodian form is *groul*, perhaps preserved in the Samre and Xong *kanoul* and the Khmous *koul*; the modern form is *prampî*=five-two. The Anamese is *bay*.

Eight.—The Mon *t'sam* seems to be formed from the same root as the Anamese, Souc, and Huei *tam*, the Stieng *pam*, and the Banar *tonam*. The old Cambodian *kati* is preserved in the Samre *katai*, and in the Xong *kati*. The modern form is *prambey*=five-three.

Nine.—This number is more variously expressed than any other in the Mon-Anam dialects. The principal forms are Mon *t'seet,* Anamese *chin*—the same root as the Samre *sen,* Banar *toxin,* Huei and Souc *kin*—and the old Cambodian *kansar,* probably akin to the Xong *kasā.* The modern Cambodian is *prambuǒn*= five-four.

Ten.—In the forms of this numeral also there are few coincidences. The Mon has *tsaŭh* or *chaŭh,* the Anamese *mu'ò'i,* the old Cambodian *ouai,* and the modern *dap.* The wild tribes, as the So, Souc, and others, seem to have adopted the Chinese root *shih* or *chi,* under the forms *chit, jit, ndjit.* In the old Cambodian for "twenty" we find *barkse,* where the second root *kse* is evidently another form for ten, and is possibly connected with the Mon *tsaŭh.*

After twenty the Cambodians have, singular to say, completely adopted the Chinese numeration up to a hundred; while the Anamese, so much more under Chinese influence, have, as well as the Mons, kept their own terms. We find the same root for "a hundred" in the Mon *mooā-klaum* and the So and Hin *mo-clam*; and it may not be impossible to connect with this the Anamese *mot tram* and the Souc and Huei *moui bam.*

Of none of the dialects mentioned in the above remarks, except the Mon, Cambodian, and Anamese, have we any grammar or any written examples. The very names of most of them were unknown until they appeared in the records of the French exploring expedition. All the materials we possess are vocabularies written down as the spoken sounds seemed to the ears of one or two particular Frenchmen. Yet with all these disadvantages, the comparison of the numerals alone throws a flood of light on the ethnology of the basin of the Mekong, and enables us to connect the remnants of the earliest occupants of that region, the rude mountain tribes, with the other members of the Mon-Anam family.

It may not be out of place again to point out that the greatest affinities are between these wild tribes and the Mons lying far to the west, with whom they could never, after both had occupied their present positions, have had any intercourse or connection. This may be naturally accounted for. The isolated hill-tribes have preserved the more archaic forms of the parent idioms, and the Mon language has been less affected by foreign influences than either of its sisters, the Anamese and Cambodian. Indeed, the modern forms of the two latter have become so corrupt that their very existence as distinct languages has been at times doubted. We thus find that roots which have been lost in the Cambodian and Anamese, and whose place has been supplied from the Chinese, are still the common property of the Mons and the hill-tribes of the Mekong.

Personal Pronouns.—In the languages of the Mon-Anam family, as amongst most Asiatic races, the original forms of the personal pronouns are overlaid by a variety of ceremonious expressions, which, taking their place, have relegated them in many instances to serve the sole purpose of expressing extreme inferiority in the person to whom they are used. In Anamese the real first personal pronoun seems to have been actually lost. There is no expression simply meaning "I," *ego*. In Mon and Cambodian the pronoun, as distinguished from the honorific equivalents substituted for it, is often only used by superiors in addressing those much below them. In such cases the employment of the personal pronoun would be a grave solecism and breach of good manners between equals or towards superiors.

The following table gives the personal pronouns:—

	Mon.	Cambodian.	Anamese.
I	*öa*	*anh*	(*toi*, lit. "servant")
Thou	*m'nĕh*	*eng, mê* *neahk, neahk-nê*	*may*
He	*nyĕh*	*nê, neang*	*no*
We	*pōōey*	*iœung*	(*chung toi*)
You	*bai* *pay*	—	(*chung*) *bay*
They	*nyeh taw*	—	(*chung*) *no*

In Cambodian the second and third persons plural are not in any way distinguished from the singular. In Mon the third person plural is formed by the addition of *taw*, the plural particle, to the third person singular. In Anamese the plural is formed throughout by prefixing the plural sign *chung* to the singular pronoun.

In all these three languages, when a personal pronoun is the object, it is placed after the verb. E.g. Mon, *nyĕh hām kāw öa*, "he told me": Cambodian, *anh mœul êng*, "I see you": Anamese, *no thu'o'ng tôi*, "he loves me." This idiom is entirely opposed to that of the Burmese, which would express the first of the foregoing sentences thus:—*nga-ko thoo pyauthee*, "me-to he told."

There are no possessive pronouns. "My," "your," "his," are expressed by one of the personal pronouns in the above table, or its honorific equivalent, placed after the thing possessed. Thus, "his house" is rendered "house he." In this also the Mon-Anam differs from the Tibeto-Burman idiom.

Relative Pronouns.—One great peculiarity of the class of languages which is sometimes designated Turanian, sometimes Mon-Aryan, is the absence of a true relative pronoun. This is generally expressed by what is called a relative participle. In the Dravidian dialects, in the Japanese, the Chinese, Tibeto-Burman, Tai, and other languages of eastern Asia, this rule holds good. Caldwell remarks: "Though the use of a relative participle, instead of a relative pronoun, is characteristic of the Scythian (Turanian) tongues, yet both the Turkish and the Finnish languages possess a relative pronoun as well. The use of such a pronoun seems foreign to the grammatical structure of those languages, and is reasonably supposed to have been imitated from the usage of languages of the Indo-European stock. It is certain that Turkish has been much influenced by Persian; and Oriental Turkish, though it has borrowed from Persian a relative pronoun, rarely uses it, and ordinarily substitutes for it an appended particle of its own in a genuinely Scythian manner."

The Mon follows the general rule, and has no sign of a relative pronoun; it expresses "he who reads the book," by *nyĕh pauh leik,* lit. "he reading book." It is, therefore, rather startling to find that the Cambodian and Anamese both possess a relative pronoun. Aymonier says: "The relative pronouns (in Cambodian) are *del* and *dâ;* ex. *menŭs del iœung chup,* 'the man whom we have met.'" Aubaret, in his "Anamese Grammar," writes: "The relative 'who' is expressed by *làké,* 'être celui qui,' ex. *anh làké da noi,* lit. 'you are he who has said,' or 'it is you who have said.' Nevertheless, the relative 'who' is more often not expressed. The relative 'that which' does not exist in Anamese, but is expressed by means of a demonstrative pronoun."

There seems little doubt, from the examples given by the above authorities, that Cambodian and Anamese possess true relative pronouns. To account for this anomaly, so opposed to the genius of the languages, is difficult. Edkins truly says: "The reason why the eastern Asiatic nations did not adopt a relative with full powers is found in the nature of their grammar. The subordinate sentence must in their languages come before the principal one. A sentence whose nominative is a relative pronoun is with them a subordinate sentence, and speech in their languages cannot expand itself by a series of subordinate or circumstantial clauses coming after that which contains the nominative and principal verb."

The Mon is in complete accordance with this law, while the Cambodian and Anamese follow in this particular the construction which obtains in the Indo-European languages; *e.g.* in Cambodian—

Khnhnôm sekâhl menus dêl peäk au khihr.
= "I know (the) man who wears (the) robe blue."

Demonstratives.—The pronoun "this" is rendered in Mon by *wŭh* and *eenaw*, and "that" by *kaw* and *tay*. In Cambodiau the demonstratives are expressed by the particles *nê*, *nô*, and *nôu*, or by the personal pronouns. In Anamese *nay*, "this," *kia* and *ay*, "that," seem closely related to the Mon forms. All these demonstrative particles are placed after the nouns to which they belong, as in the Tai; while the Tibeto-Burman idiom reverses this order.

Verb.—The verb is, in all these languages, either the simple root or a union of two simple roots, $R+R$. It possesses neither conjugation, mood, nor tense, as understood in European grammar. All the accidents which we designate by those terms are expressed by separate roots, either prefixed or affixed to the principal root, which remains entirely unaltered.

The Present tense or time is denoted by the use of the simple root.

The Past is expressed in Mon by the word *tō-ey*, "done," in Anamese by *rôi*, "done, finished," in Cambodian by *hoì*, "finished," all placed after the principal verbal root; thus, "he has gone" would be rendered "he gone done." In Anamese the word *da*, "already," is used in a similar manner, but prefixed to the verbal root; and if no personal pronoun is expressed it forms a past participle; as *da chet*, "dead."

The Future is very often shown only by the connection of the parts in the sentence; thus, "to-morrow I will go" may be simply rendered by "to-morrow I go," the adverb of time being in itself sufficient to denote the future tense. In other cases the Mon uses the particle *rong* after the verbal root, while the Cambodian prefixes *sĕm*, and the Anamese *sē*, for a similar purpose.

The Imperative is generally sufficiently expressed by the tone of the voice in using the simple root, though sometimes what may be called a natural interjection is either prefixed, as in the Anamese *hāy di,* "go," or suffixed, as in the Mon *klong hooèy,* "come."

There is properly no Passive voice. Passivity is expressed by turning the sentence and employing the active form; thus, "he is loved by his father" would be rendered by "his father loves him," "the wood is split for the fire" by "they have split wood for the fire." In Anamese the verbal roots *chiu* or *phăi,* signifying to "suffer," are sometimes used to express a passive sense; as *toi dā chiu,* lit. "I beating suffered," for "I have been beaten." A similar idiom is found in the Burmese, e.g. *ayike khan byee,* "beating suffered have," in one of the Dravidian languages (Tamil), e.g. *aḍi paṭṭân* "beating suffered," and in others of the eastern Asian languages.

The negative is expressed in Mon by the particle *hoo,* in Cambodian by *mun,* and in Anamese by *khong* placed before the verb; as *oä hoo aa* (Mon), "I am not going."

As a general rule, the object follows the verb, as in English. But in Mon, when a transitive verb is in the past tense, the object is placed between the two verbal roots, as *nyĕh rán klaër tō-ey rā,* lit. "he buy cattle done." In Cambodian the object is placed between the two roots forming a compound verb; as *iok eyvan mok,* "to bring goods," the verb "bring" being formed of two roots, *iok,* "to take," and *mok,* "to come." In Anamese, when attention is especially directed to the object, it is placed before the verb; as *sách nây dã coi rồi*, lit. "book that, I have read," for "I have read that book."

In the Mon-Anam, as in most of the east and west Himalayan languages, the verbal root, with its complements of time, place, &c., may be used as a subject and placed at the beginning of the sentence; thus, "he has gone to buy cattle in the village" is rendered by "he to buy cattle in the village, go done."

All the various accidents of the simple verbal root, its several mood-relations, potential, conditional, negative, reciprocal, causative, &c., are similarly expressed by particles which are in themselves separate roots. To enumerate all these in each dialect would here be useless.

Adverbs.—There are in the Mon-Anam languages no adverbs properly so called. The particles that are used adverbially are either nouns or verbal roots. In a sketch of this kind it is unnecessary to enumerate them. They are similarly formed in all the dialects.

Prepositions.—The employment of prepositions instead of postpositions is, as before observed, a characteristic which distinguishes the Mon-Anam from the Tibeto-Burman languages.

THE MON-ANAM RACES.

The statistical tables appended to the report on the great Indian census of 1872 show eighteen divisions of the indigenous races inhabiting the province of British Burma. Dr. Mason, in his work on "Burma," taking in the whole area of the country which lies between the Bay of Bengal and eastern Bengal on the west, and China and Siam on the east, comprising both British and Independent Burma, enumerates four national, or thirty-nine tribal divisions, together with eight more unclassed, or "miscellaneous tribes," thus making a total of forty-seven varieties of the human race.

This is but a useless and unscientific subdivision; a confusion, and not a classification. While admitting that as to some of the best-known tribes and dialects the evidence we at present possess is not conclusive, it seems possible to arrange this apparently heterogeneous mass of races under three well-marked classes and some seven sub-divisions :—

Class.	Branches.
1. Mon-Anam .	Mons, or Talains.
2. Tibeto-Burman .	Burmans. Arracan Hill Tribes. Singphos, Lee-saws, &c.
3. Shan-Karen . . .	Shans, or Tai. Sgaus. Pwos, &c.

To these, although not in Burma, yet as included, both geographically and politically, within the radius of Burman influence, we may add a fourth, or island class :—

Miscellaneous .	Andamanese. Nicobarese. Selungs.

With regard to the third, or Shan-Karen class, if it might be allowed us to coin a new term, there seems good reason to mark the deep influence exercised on it by the Chinese, or their close mutual relationship, by some such alternative term as "Sinitic." The connection between the ancient Chinese and all the western and eastern Himalayan languages, as Logan names them, is no doubt great. But the special relationship between the Chinese, the Shans and the Karens, in a linguistic, social and historic sense, calls for more decided recognition.

While endeavouring to trace out, with very feeble

lights to guide us, the prehistoric relations of the great races now occupying the Indo-Chinese peninsula, both with each other and with races of presumably common origin, it will be necessary to allude to many tribes beyond the region we are chiefly concerned with. Indeed the area to be dealt with is so vast that a careful study of the map of Asia is necessary in order to comprehend fully the arguments drawn from identities existing between these various races and from their present position. We may, for convenience' sake, roughly bring them under a few heads.

1st. Those races of India, which are generally considered as aboriginal, and designated "Kolarians."

2nd. Those which Mr. Hodgson terms the "broken tribes" of western Nipál, east of the Kali river, such as the Chepang, Kasunda, Vayu, and others.

3rd. The sub-Himalayan races, the Lhopás, Lepchas, Limbus, Murmi, Magar, Newar, Kiranti, Rodong, and many others.

4th. The great races of Tibet and High Asia, occupying the two wide plateaux between the Himalaya and the Kuen-lun range, and between this latter and the Thian Shan, and extending, as the Horpa tribe do, into Songaria, almost to the Altai mountains on the north and the Koko-nor range on the east. These are the great Tibetan, or Bhot race, the Horpa and the Sokpa, the latter ranging over the wide tract of country known to M. Polo and the early travellers as Tangút.

5th. The tribes of Sifau and the Chinese borders, the Gyarung, Thochu, Manyak and Gyami, in the mountainous country from the Koko-nor to the borders of Yün-nan, lying between the platcau of Kham and the Chinese province of Sze-chuen.

6th. The Tibeto-Burman races of Burma and the north-east frontier of Bengal.

7th. The Mon-Anam nations of Pegu and the eastern parts of Siam.

8th. The great Chinese race.

The enormous tract of country stretching southward from the great wall of China and the Desert of Gobi to the China Sea and the Indian Ocean, and eastwards from the Thian Shan and Karakorum ranges, including the southern slopes of the Himalayas, along the great western bend of the Brahmapútra river to the mouths of the Ganges, and thence to the Pacific Ocean, forms the home of all these races except the first-named. When we come to compare them, we find the Chinese character and influence so strongly developed in all, that it is impossible to ascribe it to mere chance; while it is equally difficult to believe that such influence has been exerted in historical times after their arrival in their present domiciles. Yet in almost all works on the science of language we find the Chinese isolated as if it had no connection with any other, or even omitted altogether, as in Max Müller's genealogical table of languages. Should not the opposite course be followed, and in the attempt to classify the various branches of language, should not a family be formed under some such name as "Sinitic," to include those of which we are speaking?

To proceed with the historical investigation of the origin of the races now occupying the Burman peninsula. We may imagine that the first occupants of the country were a Negrito race, of which the Mincopies of the Andaman islands and the Simangs of the Malayan peninsula are the fragmentary remains. This is a mere conjecture, for no traces of such a race can be found on the Burman mainland.

The claim to the title of autochthones seems to lie between the Mons, or Talains, and the Karens. Dr. Cross, the missionary,* who has long studied the latter people, and is intimately acquainted with their languages and traditions, urges strong arguments in their favour; but his theory supposes that when the Talains and Burmans reached their present localities, they were civilized and conquering races, whereas we have every reason to believe that they were in as primitive and barbarous a state as the Karen tribes of the present day. He says: "They, the Karens, have not to any extent adopted the religion or customs of their conquerors; nor have their conquerors adopted any of their customs. This is a sufficient proof that

* Residing at Toungoo, Burma.

the Karens have for ever been a despised race, and their customs regarded as unworthy of imitation by the races who have conquered them, *and pushed them back from their original possessions.*"

This very fact seems to point to the opposite conclusion, namely, that the Karens were an intrusive race, appearing after the spread of Buddhism and a certain degree of civilization among the lowland Talain and Burman races, who, doubtless, looked with contempt on the savage mountain tribes that gradually crept onwards down all the unoccupied mountain ranges from the northward. A very modern instance of such an intrusion occurred in the Assam valley when the Singpho race, driven westward by some pressure from behind, made its first appearance there about A.D. 1783, and formed large settlements in the Assam hills.

The Karens themselves, who have retained traditions of their origin and early history with a wonderful distinctness, place their arrival in their present mountain homes at a period not earlier than A.D. 500–600. The Mons on the contrary, whose traditional history begins abruptly about B.C. 603, possess not the most shadowy memory of any early wanderings of their race, or of their having ever occupied any other dwelling-place than their present one. There can be no question that they reached the sea-coast of Pegu before the occupation of the upper valley of the Iráwadí by the Burman race; for this latter people, who have preserved accounts, more or less reliable, of their first settlement in that locality and of the tribes they encountered in their migration, make no mention of the Mons or Talains, until some time after their arrival there, as they pushed southward below the present city of Prome.

According to the Chinese annals the countries of Anam and Tonquin, when conquered by them two hundred and fourteen years before the Christian era, were occupied by the same races as at present. If a sufficiently close connection between the Mons and the nations east of them (excluding the intrusive Siamese) can be established, as Logan presumed, we may be warranted in regarding the whole group as forming the first great wave of emigration that swept over this region.

When we endeavour to trace their route, or the date of their wanderings, we are left entirely to conjecture, or to such external evidence as we can collect. We have not even the slight assistance offered by the dim traditions of most savage tribes. The probability is that they came from the westward, and at an early date sojourned for some time in the Gangetic valley.

It is now acknowledged that prior to the irruption of the Aryans into India from the west across the Indus, the valley of the Ganges was occupied by various races of Turanian origin. Without venturing on the question of the relation between these, it is clear that the Aryan authors of the Mahábhárata distinguish two races with which the Aryans came in contact:

one of fierce, black, degraded, savage tribes whom they called Ásuras, Rákshasas, &c.; the other, a people who lived in cities and possessed wealth, and whose women were fair,* whom they termed Nágas, or serpent worshippers, and who doubtless belonged to the great Takshak, or "serpent-race" of Scythia. Under the continued pressure of the advancing Aryan invaders, these Turanian tribes were driven back, carrying before them in their turn the feeble and scattered remnants of the black aboriginal race, who were either exterminated or found a last refuge in the most inaccessible forests and mountains, where their miserable descendants may be found to this day in some of the scanty, hardly human, outcast tribes of central India.

But the Turanians to a certain extent held their ground and retained possession of the uplands, and they still form a large element of the population in many parts of India. In some cases they have lost their native language, and have adopted the religion and customs of their conquerors, so that in fact to outward appearance they are only low-caste Hindus. Large bodies of them, however, especially in the Vindyan plateau of central India, still retain their nationality, their language, and to a great extent their race purity. They are now generally classed as Kolarians, but are subdivided into several tribes, of which

* Wheeler's "History of India."

the principal and least intermixed are the Hos, Mundas and Singbhúm Kols. In spite of the influences to which they have for ages been exposed, surrounded by Aryan and mixed semi-Aryan races, their Turanian and quasi-Mongolian origin may still be distinctly traced both in their language and physical characteristics. That even their purest tribes have, however, been greatly affected by intercourse with their Hindu neighbours is shown in the fact that they have lost their native roots for several common but important words, and have adopted Hindu ones. Thus while they retain their ancient name for "sun," *singi*, derived from *singil*, "fire," the root of which is the Mongol *ghel*, they have lost the Turanian root for "moon," and use *chandu* from the Hindu *chand*. Again while keeping their native name *kula* for the "tiger" (the Mon-Anam *k'la*), they have adopted the Hindu word for the "elephant," *hathi*.

Colonel Dalton says: "If we except the Dravidian dialect spoken by the Oraons and Rajmahali hill tribes, who appear to be of comparatively recent introduction, the Kolarian or Munda language is the only pre-Aryan tongue now spoken in Bihár and Bengal proper. It has been wonderfully preserved by different tribes, some massed together, as the Munda, Santal and Bhumij, some quite isolated and far apart, who have had no communication with those named or with each other for ages. And, as the Munda or Kol language is common to so many of the tribes, that may be thus linked together; and as those who do not speak it can only converse in the language of the conquerors, it is highly probable that the Munda was at one time the spoken language of all Bihár and Bengal."

Bihár is the ancient Magadha, the cradle of Buddhism, and it has often been remarked that the sculptures at Sanchi and Buddha Gaya present not Aryan but Turanian characteristics. From Shahabad and Goruckpore to the Jyntea and Cossya hills, tradition and the evidence of ancient sepulchral monuments, broken tribes, and half-forgotten languages lead us to the conclusion that this race, which we now designate Kolarian, once formed the population of Bengal, and probably its earliest occupiers, coming in from the north-east down the valley of the Brahmapútra from some region of High Asia. Tradition tells us how the mass of the race was driven out from the Gangetic valley and found a refuge on the highlands of Chútia Nágpúr.

With this Kolarian race, scholars such as Mason, Phayre and Logan, have sought to connect more or less closely the Mons of Pegu, and with them must follow the Cambodians and Anamese.* Logan, in speaking of

* Phayre, in his "History of Pegu," distinctly asserts: "We appear then to be forced to the conclusion that the Mon or Talaing people of Pegu are of the same stock as the Kols, and other aboriginal tribes of India, who may have occupied that country before the Dravidians entered it." J. A. S. B. xlii. p. 35.

the Simang dialects of the eastern archipelago, says: "The pronouns have the peculiar forms that were current in the dialects of that branch of the Himalayan people which predominated in the Gangetic basin and its confines before the Aryans advanced into it, and which spread its language and civilization eastward till they prevailed from Guzerat to Tonquin. These pronouns and many other common vocables are still used by the Kol or Santal tribes on the Ganges, the Kgi or Kasia in the Brahmapútra basin, the Paloungs, and the Mons or Peguans on the Iráwadí, the Kambojans on the Mekong, and the Anamese on the Tonquin."

That certain affinities may be traced between the Kolarian and Mon-Anam languages is true; but when we come to compare the structure of these tongues, the radical differences are too great and important to admit for a moment of an attempt to classify them under one head, or of a supposition that the one exerted on the other more than a slight and temporary influence of contact. Still the traces of a former connection are sufficiently strong to demand some explanation; and the most rational and probable one is that the Mon-Anam nations passed on their route to their present localities through the upper valley of the Ganges, where they came in contact with the Kolarian races which then occupied it.

A singular discovery made not long ago deserves mention here, as it has been brought forward as an argument by Colonel Sir A. Phayre, to confirm the "relationship" between the Mons and Mundas. This is the discovery, in 1875, in the district of Singbhúm, Chútia Nágpúr, of several stone implements of the peculiar "shoulder-headed" type, that has always been deemed "autochthonous to the Malayan countries." All the stone implements hitherto discovered in India had been of the ordinary palæolithic type found Europe, but those now referred to* are exact facsimiles of the peculiar celts that had been supposed confined to the east of the Bay of Bengal. In Europe the peculiarities of stone implements do not so vary in different localities, that any arguments can thence be drawn as to the relation existing between tribes occupying two distant points; but the Burmo-Malayan type is so distinct and singular that when we find its facsimile in a country so widely separated from the original *venue* as Chútia Nágpúr from Pegu, we are forced to the conclusion that, during the stone epoch at least, both countries must have been occupied by kindred races. While, however, we grant this, it does not follow that the races so occupying these localities and so related were the present ones, the Kols and Mons. We know that the Kols were not the earliest inhabitants of Chútia Nágpúr; there was one race at least, the Bhooians, before them; nor is there

* Asiatic Soc. of Beng. Proc., June 1875.

any ground for supposing that when the Kols arrived in Chútia Nágpúr they were a race using stone implements, and brought such with them. While we cannot tell who, if any, were the precursors of the Mons in Pegu, there is equally little reason for assuming that they, any more than the Kols, were the fashioners of these peculiar neolithic weapons. Both people possess an indigenous name for "iron," in no way derived from the languages of their neighbours, which is at least a point in evidence that they were acquainted with its use before their arrival in their present abodes.

It may, however, be allowed that from the resemblance of these Indian and Burman celts, an argument may be drawn to support a connection between *some* races at one time inhabiting Pegu and Chútia Nágpúr. Thus, in an indirect manner, is strengthened the probability that the Mon-Anam races, in their exodus from their earliest homes in High Asia, passed through the upper valley of the Ganges, and crossing the Nága hills south of Assam, struck the head waters of the Kyendwen river,—the very route, in fact, by which the Burmese army in 1820 invaded Assam. Thence they passed down the valley of the Iráwadí to the sea-coast of Pegu, where the Mons settled; their companions, the Cambodians, Anamese, and other smaller and perhaps ruder tribes, spreading out to the eastward.

When the Mons reached the shores of the Gulf of Martaban, and probably for centuries afterwards (according to their own traditions even till the sixth century before our era), they were rude and uncivilized—little better in fact than savages. They had no national organization, no king, and no cities, but were in a condition similar to that of the Karen tribes of the present day. They did not find the country of Pegu presenting the same aspect that it now does. The great alluvial plain stretching from Martaban to Rangoon, and thence to Bassein, was still buried beneath the waters of the sea. Thatone, Pegu, Rangoon, or rather the future sites of these towns, were on the sea-coast. Syriam was an island, and the valleys of the great rivers, the Iráwadí, the Salween, and the Sittoung, offered sufficient space for the scanty population.

Hitherto we have designated these inhabitants of Pegu by their national name of Mons, but to their neighbours the Burmans, as well as to their present English rulers, they are known as Talains. We must seek the origin of this name in their own traditions.

Although Pegu has given a name to the province, to the people, and to the empire of former days, it is not the scene of the opening chapters of their history. The curtain rises suddenly on Thatone or Thatún, an ancient city lying at the foot of the range of hills that culminates in the Martaban promontory, about forty-five miles north of Martaban, and eight miles in a direct line from the *present* shore of the Gulf of Martaban. The legendary history is as follows :—

Two young princes, sons of the king of the city of Thubinga, in the country of Karanáka, in Kalinga (the ancient kingdom of Telingana, on the south-east coast of India), having renounced the world, went to live as hermits on the hills by the sea-side, near the site of the present town of Thatone. One day walking by the shore they found two eggs of a *nagá-ma* or she-dragon. These they preserved, and in process of time two boys were born from the eggs. One of the boys died, but the other, brought up by the hermits, when seventeen years old, founded the city of Thatone, and collected the people of the country into it, reigning over them under the name of Thiha Radza. As the tradition adds "that Thiha Radza reigned sixty years, and that he died in the year the Lord Gautama entered Nirvána," if we take the generally received date of this latter event, namely, B.C. 543, we have the date B.C. 603, traditionally fixed for the foundation of the city of Thatone and the commencement of the Mon or Talain kingdom and history. Another and more popular version of the tradition throws back the date some sixty or eighty years.

What we are principally concerned with is the fact that the founders of Thatone were not the aborigines of the country, in fact not Mons, but colonists from the powerful Dravidian kingdom of Telingana on the western side of the Bay of Bengal. Hence the origin of the name Talain, by which the nation was afterwards known to its neighbours, although its native appellation of "Mon" is still preserved to it by the kindred races of Siam and Anam. It is not difficult, without any distortion of facts, to read between the lines of the fable given above, a true history of the events recorded. The country of Thatone and Martaban, the southern sea-board of Pegu, was inhabited by a wild and barbarous race, the Mons. A trading colony or colonies of the civilized Dravidians of Talinga arrived on the coast, and after some little time they or their offspring by the women of the country, typified by the *nagá-ma* (*nagá* being a term commonly applied to aboriginal races), founded the city of Thatone, which geology proves to have been, as the tradition states, originally situated on the sea-coast, although a wide plain now intervenes. A certain amount of civilization spread round the new city, and when the first Buddhist teachers arrived after the third great council, B.C. 241,* the people in and around the city were prepared to receive the new faith, while the wild and unmixed inhabitants of the remote parts of the country kept to the old demon worship. As the traditionary history puts it: "When the Lord Gautama attempted to land at Martaban he was opposed and stoned by the Beloos and Náts."

* According to Gen. A. Cunningham's correction.

No further facts can be ascertained respecting this early state of things. Probably civilization gradually extended itself; and the Dravidian founders and rulers of Thatone amalgamated more closely with the Mon people round them, remaining the ruling caste, but gradually losing their identity in the mass of the people, till, except the name of Talain or Taline, by which foreigners had come to distinguish the nation, no trace of them remained. No Dravidian affinities can be discovered in the Mon language, nor in the physical characteristics of the people. The only tangible mark of a former connection with India now existing are some large granite slabs lying in the jungle covering the site of the ancient town of Thatone, which bear in high relief the image of the four-armed Vishnu, one of the hands bearing a "discus," and another a mallet. The date of these it is impossible perhaps to determine, but we know that Thatone remained a waste jungle after its destruction in A.D. 1057 by Anaurahta-men-zaw, the King of Pagán. It may then be granted that the first introduction of order and civilization among the wild autochthones of Pegu was from an Indian source. But this affords us little help towards determining the source and *stirpis origo*, of the aboriginal race itself.

Allusion has been made to the Cambodians, Anamese, and smaller tribes lying between these two nations, as the congeners and perhaps the companions of the Mons in their march from the north-west. This theory is principally founded on the evidence afforded by language, and perhaps there is little else to strengthen it. Something, however, may be found even in the childish traditions of these races when carefully examined.

Like the Mons, the Cambodians have no probable account to offer of their migration into their present locality, or of their having elsewhere possessed a polity and national existence. The speculations raised on an obscure tradition that they came from the city of Muong Rom, near Taxila, in India, may be dismissed without examination. But one legend, as given by Garnier, presents a singular coincidence in particulars and in dates with the Mon legend of the foundation of Pegu.

Garnier's account is as follows: "A l'origine, les eaux couvraient entièrement la terre du Cambodge, à l'exception d'une seule île appelée Couc Thloc, qui s'était élevée graduellement au-dessus des eaux. Le roi des serpents, Phnhéa Nakh, venait quelquefois s'y étendre au soleil; sa fille Nang Nakh aimait aussi à s'y promener dans la solitude. Prea En (Indra) la vit, fut séduit par sa beauté, et le fruit de leurs communs amours fut un bel enfant nommé Prea ket Melea. Indra voulut l'emmener avec lui dans sa céleste demeure, mais les autres dieux s'y opposèrent. Indra renvoya son fils au Cambodge en lui adjoignant sept prêtres, sept nobles, et sept brahmanes, et Prea Pus Nuca (Visvacarma) bâtit pour lui la cité d'Enthapatabouri. Le roi petit fils d'Indra et de Nang Nakh monta sur le trône vers l'an 1000 de l'ère de Bouddha.* Sous ce roi, les habitants des montagnes descendirent habiter la nouvelle ville et la terre se sécha peu à peu."†

Compare the following Mon legend: The Lord Gautama was once passing through the air with thousands of Rahans across the great sea west of Thatone (the Gulf of Martaban). At that time the sea covered all the land now occupied by the great plains of Pegu and Rangoon. Far below him, in the middle of the sea, he saw a speck of sand appearing above the water, and shining like silver. On it two *hanthas* or geese were disporting themselves. The lord smiled and prophesied that on that small speck of sand should rise a great city named Hanthawadi, the capital of a mighty empire. About a thousand years after, the sea having retired gradually, a large sand-bank or island was formed, which is the site of the present city of Pegu.

At that time a hermit named Lawma lived on the Zingyike ("Foot of God") hill, not far from Thatone. To this hill a *nagá-ma* (female dragon) came gathering fruits and flowers, in a human form, and there a

---

* A.D. 457.

† Garnier, "Exp." vol. i. p. 99.

weiza, a magician or enchanter, met her. In process of time the *nagá-ma* produced, after the manner of her race, an egg like a serpent's, and leaving it in the cave they inhabited, went back to the Nagá country. The *weiza*, on his return, seeing the egg, knew he had consorted with a *nagá-ma*, was ashamed, and fled back to the Himawonta forest (the Himalaya). The hermit Lawma found the egg, from which was produced a female child of exquisite beauty, whom he nourished and brought up. When the damsel was sixteen years of age she was married to the King of Thatone, by whom she had two sons. The two princes, being discovered to be of the dragon race, were exiled and returned to the old hermit. Having provided rafts of bamboo, the hermit sent them forth with one hundred and seventy families across the sea to the westward, to seek for the island of the golden *hanthas*, and found the long-foretold city of Hanthâwadí. After sundry adventures not necessary to be here related, the two princes, with the assistance of the Thagyá-Men (Indra) founded the city of Hanthâwadí or Pegu in 1116 of the era of Buddha, answering to our A.D. 573. Thence as a centre the Mon kingdom extended itself on all sides over the present province of Pegu.

Although the Mons and Cambodians are not alone among the Indo-Chinese nations in thus attributing the fabulous origin of their princes to the Nagá or dragon race, yet there are points of resemblance in these two legends, and a strange closeness in dates that are very striking. They both point to an Indian origin for the civilization of the two nations, whose national existence seems to have begun much about the same time.

M. Garnier, in his interesting and exhaustive account of the eastern nations of Indo-China, has endeavoured, but apparently without much success, to determine the question of the origin of the ancient Khmers or Cambodians. He at all events proves historically that between the third and sixth centuries of our era they dominated the whole southern part of the country bordering on the gulf of Siam, to the Salween river on the west, thus marching with the Mons on the opposite bank of that river. He even infers that about this time their empire included the country of Pegu. That there existed close and intimate relations between the two nations is certain. The Tai or Shan race had not yet made their way down from the north, and the Mons and Cambodians possessed the whole sea-board of the gulfs of Martaban and Siam. That such close connection and intercourse *may* have sufficed to produce the resemblances in the languages of these two people, without the existence of any actual affinity between them, is possible; that it is also probable is not so easy to believe. But we find that the verbal roots common to the Mon and Anamese are still more numerous, and this is the more singular as the Anamese is often declared to be a dialect of the Chinese. So Aubaret describes it: "La langue vulgaire parlée dans le royaume d'Annam est un dialecte du chinois." Max Müller says: "The language now spoken in Cochin-China is a dialect of Chinese, at least as much as Norman French was a dialect of French, though spoken by Saxons at a Norman court. There was a native language of Cochin-China, the Annamitic, which forms, as it were, the Saxon of that country on which the Chinese, like the Norman, was grafted." *

This "native residuum of Cochin-Chinese," as the learned professor calls it, is then the ancient Annamitic language which we find offers strange resemblances in its roots to the Mon.

The history of Anam is fairly known to us through the Chinese annals from the second century before the Christian era, and there is no reason to suppose any close intercourse ever existed between the countries of Pegu and Anam, while the national individuality of the Anamese has been almost destroyed by Chinese influence. These facts strengthen the linguistic evidence of an affinity between the two peoples.

Besides the Cambodian and Anamese races, there are several wilder and more primitive tribes inhabiting the mountainous parts of the interior lying between the two countries. Of these M. Garnier writes: "Sans

---

* "Science of Language," ii. 29.

aucun doute, on retrouverait dans le langage des nombreuses tribus qui habitent encore dans la partie montagneuse du Cambodge, les sources mêmes de la langue primitive des autochthones. Les Samre, les Xong, les Khamen-boran sont de toutes ces tribus celles qui se rapprochent le plus des Khmers actuels. Leur langue est, pour les sept dixièmes, le cambodgien moderne; on n'y trouve plus aucun radical malais ou pali, non plus que la numeration quinquennale, mais en revanche un assez grand nombre de mots essentiels leur sont communs avec l'annamite.* Les Halang, les Banar, les Cedang, les Huéi, les Cat, les Souc qui habitent entre le grand fleuvre et la chaîne de la Cochinchine diffèrent davantage des Cambodgiens et leurs dialectes représentent sans doute plus fidèlement la langue des anciens autochthones."

It is then singular that among these isolated and primitive tribes we find, in many cases, the forms of roots which the more civilized Cambodian has lost, or which approach more nearly to the Mon than to the Cambodian. We have not, and can hardly at present expect to have, any knowledge of the grammatical structure of these wild tongues, seeing that it is but a very few years ago that we obtained—thanks to the labours of the French expedition—any vocabularies, or indeed any knowledge at all of some of them. We

---

* "Exolor.," i. p. 111.

must therefore make use of what we have, and endeavour to erect a structure of theoretical speculation, even though we know that those who come after will destroy much of it, and replace it with better material on a surer foundation.

Max Müller, in his "Letter on the Turanian Languages," has carefully discussed and explained the position that the first ten numerals hold in the comparison of various dialects. Leaving the full vocabularies for consideration together with the grammatical structure of these languages, it will be interesting to compare their numerals, especially with reference to their geographical position.

The first group given in the accompanying tables consists of the three great languages, the Mon, Cambodian, and Anamese, with those of three of the savage tribes dwelling between Cambodia and Anam. It will hardly be denied that the roots of the first four numerals are the same in all these dialects.

	1 Mon.	2 Cambod. (anc.)	3 Anam.	4 Xtieng.	5 Banar.	6 Souc and Huei.
One	mooä	monay	môt	mou oi	moin	moui
Two	bä	bar	hai	bar	bar	bar
Three	pe	peh	ba	pey	peng	pe
Four	paun	pon	bôn	pouôn	ponon	pouôn
Five	m'son	pram	nam	pram	po-dam	soung
Six	t'ron	krong	sau	prao	to-tron	treou
Seven	t'pauh	groul	bay	po	to-po	pho
Eight	t'sam	kati	tam	pam	to-nam	tam
Nine	t'seet	kansar	chin	sou	to-xin	kin
Ten	t'sauh	ouai	mu'ôï	giemat	ming jit	chit

	7 Chinese.			8 Mi	9 Mou-tse	10 Khos.	11 Lolos.	12 Kato.
One	yih	ih	chit	moue	te-ma	ti	ti-leu	teu-ko
Two	i	ni	nng	bar	ni-ma	nhi	nhi-leu	nhe-ko
Three	san	sam		pe	che-lé	soung	sa-leu	se-ko
Four	sre	sz	si	si	ho-le	he	fe-leu	li-ko
Five	wu	'ng	go	ha	nga-ma	nga	ngo-leu	ngo-ko
Six	lak	luh	liu	oc	ko-ma	ko	tohou-leu	tcho-ko
Seven	t'sih	ch'i	ch'it	chet	seu-ma	si	che-leu	se-ko
Eight	pah	pat	peh	pet	hi-ma	his	he-leu	he-ko
Nine	kiu	chiu	kaw	kao	ho-ma	hueu	kou-leu	ki-ko
Ten	shih	shap	seh	sip	te-chi	che	tseu-leu	tse-ko

We then find that the Cambodian and Anamese differ as to the rest of the numerals from the Mon and from each other, nor do they seem to owe anything to a Chinese derivation. But in the three savage and more primitive dialects we find further traces of resemblance to the Mon. Thus, the Souc and Huei have "five" *soung*, "six" *treou*, "seven" *pho*, "eight" *tam*, corresponding to the Mon *m'son*, *t'rou*, *t'pauh*, *t'sam*; the Banar has "six" *to-trou*, "seven" *to-po*, "eight" *to-nam*; the Xtieng has "six" *prao*, "seven" *po*, "eight" *pam*. These may be said to be mere coincidences, but it appears to be more difficult and unreasonable to think them such, than to believe that they show a real connection between these dialects and the Mon, or perhaps rather that they are evidence of a language common to all these cognate races before they became politically and dialectically divided.

At all events we have here these languages of petty wild tribes showing singular resemblances in their common numerals to the language of a distant nation with which it is pretty certain those tribes have never had any intercourse or connection, and differing from the languages of the neighbouring races under whose influence they have been for centuries both socially and politically placed.

The second group contains the numerals of those tribes which exhibit more or less affinity with the Chinese. These are naturally those lying to the northward, near the Chinese frontier. One of them, the Mi, is an example of several others, which combine the results of both Cambodian and Chinese influence, the first three numbers being Cambodian or Mon-Anam, and the others more or less derived from the Chinese. The remaining dialects exhibit in their numerals a direct descent from the Chinese roots, in some instances showing Tibeto-Burman affinities, as in the numerals "five" and "six."

Until we obtain further knowledge of these wild hill-tribes, far more interesting in a scientific point of view than their mixed and more civilized neighbours, we can only form opinions on the slight evidence before us; and when we find it altogether on one side, we are surely warranted, until it is contradicted, in accepting the conclusion to which it leads us. This conclusion seems to be that in early ages the country lying east of the Iráwadí river, along the whole sea-board to the China sea, was occupied by kindred tribes to whom Logan has given the appropriate name of the Mon-Anam race. We shall see how far a comparison of the structure and vocabulary of the languages confirms this supposition.

THE SHOULDER-HEADED CELTS OF BURMA.

I PRETEND to no scientific knowledge of palæolithic implements, and therefore cannot venture to draw any conclusions from the few facts I offer respecting the peculiar class of stone celts found in Burma.

There is, I believe, very little difference in the types of stone implements belonging to Europe, and those generally discovered in India up to 1875. It was not, indeed, till A.D. 1861 that the existence of stone weapons in India was known. But a peculiar and entirely different type has been for some time known as belonging to the Malayan peninsula. I am not aware if it is generally understood by archæologists at home that this peculiar type has a much wider range.

First to describe the implement itself, and show in what it differs from the ordinary stone implement of Europe. From the diagrams, giving a front and side view, it will be seen that the peculiarities are in the "shoulders" it possesses, and in the edge being ground down on *one* side like a chisel, instead of on both sides like an axe, as is usually the case.

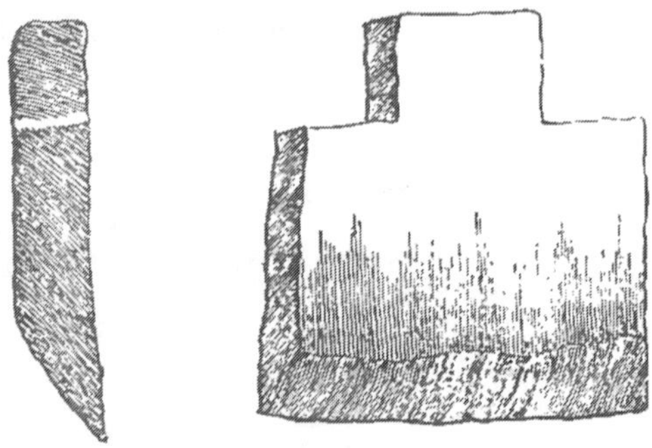

This type is that which is generally found not only in the Malayan peninsula but also in the lower part of Burma, forming the provinces of Pegu and Tenasserim. In 1875 the same type of stone implement was discovered in the district of Chutiá Nágpúr, in central India, and figured in the Journal of the Bengal Asiatic Society, for June 1875. A prehistoric ethnological connection between the Malay peninsula, the southern sea-board of Burma, and the opposite eastern coast of India seems to be thus pointed out. Whether any further addition to the range of these peculiar stone weapons will in time be made, remains to be seen.

The Burmese celts seem to be composed of a fine-grained slate, common in several parts of the country. They are generally found on the hill sides; for the great rice-producing plains of Pegu and the Burman littoral have only been raised above the waters of the Gulf of Martaban in what we may deem the historic age, and were never occupied by a stone implement using race. The larger number of specimens as yet obtained of Burmese celts are of such small size as to cause wonder to what use they could have been put, though a few very large oues have been found.

It is strange to find the same superstitions connected with these implements in Burma as in England, in Brittany, in Finland, in China and in Brazil.* The Burman name for them is *mo-gyo*, "thunderbolt" (literally "cloud or sky chain"), and the belief of the natives is that whenever a flash of lightning strikes the earth one of these stones falls with it, buries itself in the earth, and makes its way after three years agaiu to the surface, where it may be found. The other superstitious ideas connected with these celts are many. Their medicinal virtues are supposed to be great, though in what particular respect is not quite ascertained; but it is very difficult to obtain a perfect specimen from the natives; they are all more or less chipped, particles having been taken off from time to time, ground down, and mixed with medicine. The copper celts are even more valued in this respect. The three-angled specimen in my collection I bought from

* Tylor, "Early Hist., p. 226."

a native doctor for £1 10*s*. It is believed that if a plantain tree be cut down and a "thunderbolt" laid on the germinal shoot, it will not spread again. A house in which one of these stones is kept will be safe from lightning and from fire. It acts as a charm in protecting the wearer from sword and bullet wounds.

LIFE OF GAUTAMA.

On no subject, perhaps, connected with the history of long past ages, has so large a literature accumulated within a few years as on that of Buddhism, and its founder, Gautama Sákya Buddha. During the first quarter of the present century the attention of Orientalists was chiefly directed to the study of Sanskrit, Zend, and Egyptian antiquities; and little, if anything, was really known of a religion and a literature which, ancient as they are, remain to this day living facts for three hundred and sixty-nine million souls, or more than a third part of the earth's inhabitants.

It was not till the discovery in 1824 by Bryan H. Hodgson, of a vast mass of Sanskrit Buddhist literature existing in Nípal, and unknown to the learned world of Europe, that the curiosity and attention of scholars was aroused; and since that date Buddhism has been carefully studied, under its various aspects, in Ceylon, Tibet, China, and the Indo-Chinese countries. Unfortunately both the ethics of Buddhism, and the personal history of its founder are still matters on which students entertain the most divergent opinions.

As a religious system Buddhism has been derived from Brahmanism, from Judaism, and from Christianity; and its doctrines have been interpreted in the most opposite senses. The era of Gautama Buddha has been variously fixed from B.C. 2400 to 370, Professor H. H. Wilson even doubting if such a personage ever really existed.

In an age of philosophic enquiry such scepticism is only what may be expected, and it has at least one advantage over the old faith in ancient traditions, that it affords room for speculation and unfettered research, which *may* lead to the discovery of surer lights. Following such landmarks as we find scattered here and there, as the mariner making his way in ancient times, without a compass, from point to point, not, it may be, by the truest or shortest route, at last reached the end of his voyage, so we may, while omitting, or even misrepresenting some minor intermediate details, construct from the salient points of history a sufficiently accurate account of the origin and progress of Buddhism.

This great religious system has not only exercised an enormous influence over a great portion of the human race, but has ever had a singular attraction for the European students of its mysteries. St. Hilaire in his "Le Bouddha," published in 1859, says: "Je n'hésite pas à ajouter que, sauf le Christ tout seul, il n'est point, parmi les fondateurs de religion, de figure plus pure ni plus touchante que celle du Bouddha." The learned Danish professor, Fausböll, writes, in 1872: "The more I learn to know Buddha the more I admire him, and the sooncr all mankind shall have been made acquainted with his doctrines the better it will be, for he is certainly one of the heroes of humanity."*

That Buddhism arose in India, and is in some way connected with Brahmanism, may be taken as a concise summary of the popular idea on the subject. Learned works on the subject, though accessible, only attract a certain class of the now large and ever-increasing reading public, and moreover, being out of date, that is to say, published some few years ago, are nearly as unknown as works of the last century.

To arrive at any just idea of the origin of Buddhism we must go far back, to a period of which we indeed know little historically, but on which much speculative learning has been expended. What we do know is, that northern India, to use a general expression, was peopled at some unknown date by an Aryan immigration of a race kindred to, in fact an offshoot of, the Iranian or Persian branch of the Indo-European family.

Notwithstanding the common use, in these days, of the expression "our Aryan brethren," it may be safely assumed that not a third of those who write, or of

* "Ten Játakas," preface, p. viii.

those who read it, have any other idea of its meaning than that the Hindoos—by which they mean the *whole* or nearly the whole of the inhabitants of India—are in some way ethnologically allied to Europeans. This is, however, by no means the case. The Aryans of India were the last, and not the most numerous of the successive waves that flowed into the peninsula. Without venturing into ethnological discussions on the affinities of this or that particular people, it may be generally asserted that India, in the very earliest times, was peopled by races who belonged to the Turanian, or at least to a non-Aryan, branch of the human family.

That the Indian Aryans and the ancient Persians were brethren in blood and in faith we have had undoubted proof, and the science of comparative philology teaches us that they both claim relationship with the Aryan races of Europe. Dr. Muir says: "The Sanskrit, Zend, Greek and Latin, are all as it were sisters, daughters of one mother who died in giving them birth. All races of men who spoke these languages are also descended from one stock, separated by migration, their ancestors at a very remote period living in some country out of India, and speaking one language." (Sanskrit Texts, ii.)

Although affording no chronological information, the ancient poems and songs of these Aryan immigrants present us with vivid pictures of their social condition.

These songs, handed down through generations of bards, and afterwards collected under the title of the "Rig-Veda," have only lately been made accessible to European scholars. From them we learn that when the Aryans, pouring through the passes of the Hindu Koosh, occupied the plains of the Panjáb or Five Rivers, they were simply a warlike tribe, possessing much in common with their European kindred. They knew not caste, they had no temples or representations of their deities; Brahma, Siva, and Vishnu, and the whole paraphernalia of Brahmanism existed not for them. In the earliest poems the Brahmans themselves are unmentioned. The Vedic Aryans are only known among themselves as the Kshatriyas, the "Freemen" or "Warriors," and the Rishis or "Bards."

Their great deities were Súrya, the Sun-god, of whom another conception was Agni, "Fire," Indra, the great ruler of the sky, Varuna, the deity of water, Ushas, the Dawn, and many other deified embodiments of the elements and powers of nature. We know that the religion which Zoroaster introduced among the Persians was but a reformation and refinement of a still more ancient worship of Mithra, the Sun-god, and the elemental spirits. And we find in the singular dualistic system of the Zendavesta, several of the Vedic deities, although in some cases they have ceased to be gods, and have become the ministers of Ormuzd or Ahriman. Thus we find Vayu, the Wind-god of both Persians and Indians, one of the angels of Ormuzd, the Creator; but, on the contrary, Indra, the great Vedic king of heaven, is, in the Persian mythology, transformed into one of the six evil angels of Ahriman, the Principle of Evil. This goes to show that the separation between these two branches of the Aryan family took place before the reformation of Zoroaster.

The Kshatriyas and Rishis lived together, worshipping the same gods, but with different rites; the former sacrificed horses and oxen, poured out libations of strong drink, and feasted like the hero sons of Woden, in honour of their deities, while the peaceful Rishis offered fruits, flowers and milk, and sang hymns of praise and invocation.

Their ideas of a future state seem to have been much the same as those which the Scandinavian races brought from their common ancestral home. While the higher and more spiritual hymns express a dim belief in a righteous judgment, and an undefined system of reward and punishment, belonging probably to the more elevated and refined ideas of the bardic class; the popular conception was of a heaven ruled by Indra and his spouse, the chief delights of which consisted in unending feasting and drinking in the company of the celestial nymphs, a close version of the Valhalla feasts and the Valkyrias of our northern ancestors.

There is not the slightest trace of the doctrine of the metempsychosis, which afterwards became, and still is, a distinguishing feature of all the religions of India. The religion was, moreover, patriarchal in its rites. The father was, as in all early times, the priest of the family; for although the Rishis seem to have been distinguished, and even honoured, for their superior piety, refinement, and perhaps learning, there is no proof that they made any claims as a separate priestly class. The peculiar sanctity and miraculous knowledge attributed to them in after times were only the inventions of the Brahmans.

It is therefore clear that the early religion of the Vedic Aryans had nothing in common with Brahmanism, but was even opposed to its tenets; and probably the Brahmans themselves were unknown until the Aryans advanced beyond the Panjáb, into the valleys of the Jumna and Ganges.

At what date this important event took place it is impossible to conjecture; but the establishment of the Aryans in the centre of Gangetic India brought them into close comtact with the Brahmans, and with the non-Aryan races—a contact destined to exert the most serious influence on their character, both in religious and social matters. It must be borne in mind that even yet the Brahmans had obtained no pre-eminence; they were simply a priestly class of sacrificers, and were deemed inferior to the Kshatriyas, or warriors. This is clearly shown in the great Mahábhárata epic, where the prince, Arjuna, disguised as a Brahman, having won the fair prize of the great archery tournament, the hand of the princess Draupadí, is assailed with invective and then with blows, on account of the presumption of the supposed Brahman in daring to mingle as an equal among Kshatriya youths, and aspire to the hand of a Kshatriya maiden. But from this we can perceive that the priestly influence of the Brahmans was gaining ground among the Aryan race. They had by degrees become the only sacrificers and celebrants of the sacred rites, the sole ministers between earth and heaven. Still more significant fact, in these later times, the great deities of the primitive Aryans, Agni, Indra and others, had fallen into a secondary place in the Vedic Pantheon, and given place to a new god, or at least to a new conception of the deity, Brahman, or Brahmá, the creator and soul of the universe, a character unknown to the early Kshatriya and Rishi tribes. Brahmá was emphatically the deity of the Brahmans, who claimed to issue from his mouth. With this new dcity arose a new stage of religious development; with the priest came the ideas of sacrifice, of atonement for sin, of penance, and of priestly propitiation, all unknown in the early Vedic hymns. It may perhaps startle some readers who have been accustomed to associate Brahmanism—the Hindu religion—with the most scrupulous dread and abhorrence of taking life, to learn that the chief duty of the Brahmans in early days was to sacrifice oxen, horses and other animals to the gods, and that animal sacrifices were only forbidden and put down by a Buddhist king, after the era of Alexander the Great.

Next was developed the doctrine of the metempsychosis, also unknown to the primitive religion of the Aryan settlers. This belief seems to have been an outcome of the reveries and spiritual aspirations of the Brahman sages, the austere and mystic recluses, who formed quite a different class from the ordinary priests and sacrificers. It does not appear to have made much way or had much influence on the popular religion.

Who and what the Brahmans themselves originally were is still a matter of learned discussion. Their own claims to be the descendants of the ancient Rishis, and to have always held the pre-eminent position they have since attained, are utterly false. They formed no part of the great Aryan colonization of the Panjáb. Their home was eastwards in central India, and they seem to have been in more or less intercourse and alliance with the Nága races, the dark non-Aryan possessors of the soil, who were everywhere the foes and opponents of the fair Aryan invaders. That the Brahmans were themselves Aryans is undoubted; but what their position or quality originally was, is a mystery. How did they come in advance of the great Aryan migration? Whence did they acquire their superior learning and metaphysical doctrines. What were their relations to the original non-Aryan people, who were ultimately driven out or conquered by the advancing Aryans? These are questions which afford scope for ingenious speculation, but the answers to which must in any case be doubtful.

As the Aryan invaders filled the fertile valleys of the Ganges and Jumna, and finally established their empire in central India, with the great city of Páṭaliputra (the modern Patna) as the capital, they had come more and more into collision with the non-Aryan inhabitants, who were styled generally, in the Vedic epics, Nágas. Some fled, others remained to be the serfs and bondsmen of the conquerors; and here we have the origin of that system of "caste," which has been looked on as the peculiar feature of Brahmanism, as the result and development of a certain *religious system.* In truth, it was originally nothing more than the distinction between the conquerors and the conquered, of which we have examples in other nations, as, for instance, the freemen and the helots of Sparta. Doubtless, as the priestly Brahman class gained influence, they saw the means of increasing their power, by adding all the sanction of religion to what had been merely a political expedient. They fostered the pride of the warlike Kshatriyas, their supporters, by claiming for the two classes of pure Aryan blood, the warriors and the priests, a haughty and unapproachable superiority over the Sudras, that is, all the aboriginal non-Aryan population. We may be sure that the wily priesthood only gradually put forward their own claim to take the first rank; and we know that it was not at first allowed them, for in the laws of the great mythical law-giver Manu, the Brahmans rank next below the Kshatriyas in the enumeration of the castes.

That this is the origin of caste is further shown by the fact that, according to the accounts given by the Greek historians of Alexander's time, caste did not exist among the pure Aryan population of the Panjáb. The marriage customs, as related by Strabo, would alone prove this. He says that the maidens were given in marriage to the victors in friendly contests in running, wrestling and feats of arms; a truly Aryan custom, and such as was practised in the early Vedic times, but utterly incompatible with the idea of caste. Moreover, Strabo mentions the fact that two of the Brahmans partook of food at Alexander's table. Compare this with the account of the social system existing in the Gangetic empire of Magadha, written by Megasthenes, some fifteen years after the death of Alexander. That also was an Aryan kingdom, established by the Aryan Kshatriyas, the same race as the men of the Panjáb, whom Alexander conquered. There also we find Brahmans, the brethren of Kalanos and Mandanis, whose sayings to Onesikritos, the friend of Alexander, are recorded by Strabo. But the people of this kingdom are divided into castes, out of which the members may not marry. The agricultural class, distinct from the military, only toiled as the slaves of the sovereign. The Brahmans, Megasthenes tells us, were the highest in rank of all the castes. It is evident that the state of society, modified as it was, we must remember, by the increasing influence of Buddhism, which is a practical protest against all caste, was, in central India, very different from that which had been presented to the observation of Alexauder's companions in the Panjáb some fifteen years previous. We cannot imagine that this difference arose in those fifteen years; and if caste and its social trammels were an inherent part of ancient Brahmanism as a religious element, or of the social condition of the Aryan colonists of northern India, how comes it that we find no trace of it in their earliest settlements, and among what we mnst consider the purest branch of the race? On the contrary, we find it where the Aryans held the position of conquerors, and the mass of the population that of conquered, and where a priestly class, siding with the dominant power at first, had, by the influence of superior learning and of the powers of superstition, usurped for themselves an almost divine position, which they upheld by a system, the most perfect ever devised for degrading and enslaving the human soul and intellect. It is surely not too much to draw the rational conclusion that the Hindoo caste system arose as a political expedient for keeping in subjection a conquered race, and at first only marked—as the Sanskrit word for it, *varna*, "colour," indicates—a distinction of race, between the fair Aryan lords, and their dark non-Aryan serfs.

Central India presented then, six centuries before Christ, a gloomy and melancholy picture:—the masses politically crushed and oppressed by a haughty and powerful alien military class; in turn, the masters and bondsmen, both subject to the spiritual domination of an arrogant priesthood, who had gradually imposed the fetters of a cruel and degrading superstition on all classes, on prince and noble, soldier and peasant. They alone, they taught, were the pure offspring and ministers of the deity; all others, whatever their social rank, were but as dust beneath the feet of the "twice born" Brahman. The religion they inculcated had long since departed from the simple faith and the worship of the elements, which the Vedic Aryans had brought from their ancestral trans-Himalayan home. An elaborate ritual of ceremony and sacrifice, the knowledge of which was confined to themselves, and in which they were the sole efficient hierophants, was put forward as the only means of gaining the favour, or appeasing the wrath of the gods. This ritual demanded the sacrificial slaughter of thousands of animals, while on the other hand the doctrine of transmigration taught that each of these victims might contain the soul of one who had been nearest and dearest to the worshipper. And the result of all this—what was it? Endless transmigrations, and the continued seeking in each new birth to acquire, by the most cruel and painful austerities, such a measure of purity and virtue as to ensure in the next existence the opportunity of acquiring more; and thus through an infinite, ever-widening series of existences, like the gradually fading circles on a still pool, the soul, purified from the disturbing influence of earthly passions and feelings, is insensibly lost in the all-prevading essence of Brahman. Truly a dim and dreary goal for the weary soul to look forward to. But even this path was not plain and defined. The metaphysical subtleties of the Brahman sages, had divided them into apparently six great and diametrically opposite schools. One of these taught the existence and agency of numberless genii, whose favour it was alone necessary for man to propitiate, as the authors of all happiness or misery. The second denied the dogma of metempsychosis, and maintained that every being had the innate power of reproducing, by way of generation, another being of similar nature. The third held that man had his beginning in the womb of his mother, and that death was the end and destruction of his being. The fourth taught that all beings had neither beginning nor end, and that there existed no influence of good or bad deeds. The fifth defined Nirvána to be a long life like that of the Devas and Brahmas, saw no harm in the killing of animals, and asserted the existence of a state of reward and punishment. The last school boldly taught the existence of a supreme being, creator of all that exists, and alone worthy of receiving adoration.* Amidst this social degradation and this chaos of creeds, we may believe the Hindu mind looked around for some guide and deliverer. Doubtless the myths contained in the Buddhist books, setting forth the universal expectation through all the spiritual worlds of the Devas, and among the holy Rishis or Brahman sages, of the coming of the great Bodhisatwa, who should become the Buddha,

> "Able to save and deliver the world of men,
> From the deep sea of misery and grief,"

were but the expression of the feeling of unrest and longing that animated the whole of Gangetic Hindustan. Be this as it may, there remains the undoubted fact that when Gautama appeared, he experienced little of the opposition and neglect that the founders of new religions generally encounter. Unlike Mohammed, who is said to have made thirteen converts in the first three years of his mission, Gautama, even allowing for all exaggeration in the Buddhist accounts, attracted thousands of disciples from the beginning of his career. Nor will this seem strange when we come to contrast the teaching he offered with that of the old religion.

---

* Bigandet, "Life of Gaudama."

Mill describes Gautama as the "philosophical opponent of popular superstition, and Brahmanical caste." A more valuable opinion is that of one of the most enlightened living native scholars of India, Baboo Rajendralala Mitra. He says: "Buddhism rose mainly by working on the religious sentiment of the people. . . At a time when the rituals of the Vedic worship deluged the country with the blood of thousands of animals slaughtered in the name of God, the universal benevolence of Sákya appealed to the feelings of the people with a force and directness of purpose which proved irresistible. No man who had seen a dozen head of cattle killed by spikes driven into their chests, the usual mode of sacrifice at the time, could for a moment deny the superiority of a religion which preached mercy for all created beings, and absolutely prohibited slaughter of every kind."*

As every successful reformer is in himself but the typical expression of the hopes, the fears, the doubts, the aspirations, seething in the minds of the people among whom he appears, but remaining inarticulate until the mass find, as it were, in him a voice through which to make themselves heard, so we shall find in the recorded doubts and mental struggles through which Gautama perfected his doctrine, the best expression of the heart and feelings of central India at this period.

* "The Antiquities of Orissa," Part i.

There is no need, in connection with this subject, to attempt to fix the exact date of Gautama's appearance, nor to consider the narratives, many of them evidently fabulous additions of after days, connected with his birth and early life. Suffice it to say that all the probabilities place the first event in the sixth century before Christ. Stripped of its marvellous and fictitious surroundings, the well-known story of the youthful prince abandoning his palace, his wife and his infant child, to search for wisdom and deliverance from the mental misery and doubt which oppressed his soul, is no doubt true in its main features. The Buddhist legends relating the miraculous way in which he was gradually led on to this final resolve, may be taken as poetical myths embodying certain psychological developments. We are now concerned with him as the philosophic student seeking to solve the doubts and mysteries he finds within himself.

Scattered throughout the whole legendary history of the life of Gautama Buddha, we find such genuine, natural incidents as in themselves prove the actual entity of the great teacher. Here was no deified Avatára proclaiming a new cultus, such as Brahmanism frequently presents, but a human being struggling amid all the shadows and the aspirations of the human soul upwards towards the light. Had Gautama not really existed he would have been for the Buddhists only what the Brahmans afterwards made him,* an *avatára* or incarnation of some previous deity, who appeared on earth to reform the abuses that had crept into religion. He would never have been presented in the sacred books as a learner before he became a teacher.

No sooner had Gautama forsaken his princely state, resolved to find the means of deliverance from the evil he saw around him, than he betook himself to the austere Brahman recluses who, amidst forests and deserts, by rigorous penances and abstraction from all worldly concerns, sought and professed to arrive at that perfect purity which led towards final absorption into the divine essence. These were the teachers whom the young prince had been taught to regard as having obtained a knowledge of the supreme wisdom, and to them he at once goes and seeks admission as a disciple.

For some time, the history of his life relates, he listened to their doctrines, and observed their ceremonial rites. But his soul was not satisfied. He addressed his master thus: "I perceive that your system, although it promises the reward of heaven to certain persons, yet provides no means of final deliverance;

"You give up all, friends, relatives, and worldly delights,
And suffer pain that you may be born in heaven;
Not considering that after being thus born on high,
In future years you may return and be born even in hell."

* In later times the Brahmans fabled Buddha to have been the ninth *avatára* of Vishnu.

The Brahmans asked what fault he found with their religious discipline, and then ensued this discussion.

Gautama answered: "You afflict yourselves to-day with every kind of mortification, and hereafter again you will return into this very condition that you now hope to escape from."

They replied: "This very pain we suffer gives us assurance and peace! There is great merit attaching to it, and we are confident that by this religious discipline we shall get rid of these ungainly bodies of ours, and obtain beautiful and excellent shapes elsewhere."

"And yet what assurance have you," said Gautama, "that, after obtaining the excellent and beautiful bodies of which you speak, you have escaped the necessity of returning to the same condition you are now in? What assurance have you that you have for ever got rid of sorrow?"

They replied: "Not so; it does not follow that we shall hereafter return to sorrow; for the express purpose of our present discipline is, that we may secure happiness as a certainty."

Gautama answered: "But there is no wisdom in this; for would a wise man seek for something apparently profitable if he knew that it involved, as a cousequence, future loss? Would this be the work of wisdom?"

The Brahmans replied: "You have but a partial knowledge of our system. In days gone by, countless holy men practised this method of self-discipline in this very place. Countless Rishis of regal birth—myriads of such persons—by undergoing these mortifications sought to attain to future bliss."

"Gautama said: "A thousand myriad years, perhaps you would say! Alas! alas! what deceptive speech; for where is the promise of escape in the end? The future joy involves the necessity of birth and death, and therefore of future misery."

The Brahmans continued: "The monarch of this region, desiring to make an inviolable compact, sacrificed to the gods countless victims of various kinds, hoping hereafter to attain the happiness of heaven."

Gautama answered: "This system of religion, which consists in offering up sacrifices slain by the hand of those engaged in it—tell me, what is the character of this system?"

They replied: "It is a custom which has been handed down from very remote time, that those who worship the gods should do it in this way."

Gautama asked: "How can the system which requires the infliction of misery on others be called a religious system? Surely if the body were polluted and filthy it would not be made pure or clean by returning again to the filth and rolling in it? How, then, having a body defiled with blood, will the shedding of blood restore it to purity? To seek a good by doing an evil is surely no safe plan."

The Brahmans answered: "This, nevertheless, is a true system of religion."

Gautama said again: "But in what way, and by what reason?"

They replied: "According to the Vedas, and what we find the old Rishis said. The system is simply this, that all men who worship the gods must sacrifice."

Gautama said: "I will ask you, then, if a man in worshipping the gods sacrifice sheep, and so does well, why should he not kill his child, his relative, or dear friend, in worshipping the gods, and so do better. Surely there can be no merit in killing a sheep. It is but a confused and illogical system, this."

After this he tells these sages that there would be no peace for him in the pursuit of their aim, and that he must go elsewhere and seek for a more complete release.

Here we have presented to us an exposition of the revolt of the human heart against the horrible system of penance and cruel austerities inculcated by the Brahmanical system as an essential part of religion and the only means of salvation.

Gautama next proceeds to the retreat of one of the greatest Brahman hermit sages, and seeks instruction from him. This philosopher teaches him to seek, through self-denial and contemplation, absorption into the Eternal Creative Essence, Ísvara (or Íswara). Gautama objects to creation by Ísvara, because then there could be no succession of events, no causes of sorrow, no variety of gods; but all men would regard Ísvara as their father—there could be no disputes about this very subject, whether Ísvara exists or not—in short, if Ísvara created all things, then all things must have been good, and there could have been no possibility of evil.

"I seek," he continues, "a condition of escape that admits of no return to life and its troubles;" on which the Brahman insists that his system teaches this.

"But how?" inquires Gautama. "At one moment you speak of your discipline leading to a definite condition of being, and the next you say it admits of no return; this is strange."

"And so it is," said the sage; "for this condition of which I speak is that of the great Brahmá, whose substantial existence is one of perfect quietude, without beginning, without end; without bounds or limits, no first or last, his operations inexhaustible, his form without parts or marks—immutable, incorruptible."

"But if this be so," replied Gautama, "what becomes of him, and who is he when, at the end of the Kalpa,* this heaven and earth, even up to the abode of Sakra, is burnt up and entirely destroyed; where, then, is your creator?"

The Brahman then asked his questioner what system of deliverance he sought.

* A cycle of existence.

To which Gautama replied: "I seek a system in which questions about the elements shall have no place, in which there shall be no discussion about the senses or their objects, no talk of death or birth, disease or old age, no questioning about existence or non-existence, about eternity or non-eternity, in which words shall be useless, and the idea of the boundless and illimitable realized but not talked about."

This passionate outcry for something defined, some fixed and sure standing-point amidst the tossing sea of metaphysical doubts and theories, would have led, one would think, a mind so noble, so pure, and so intellectual as that of Gautama must have been, to take refuge in a conception of an all-powerful Providence, at least as clear as that attained to by the great Greek thinkers. But there is great reason to believe that the mystery of the existence of evil in the creation of a Supreme Creator, was to him an insurmountable obstacle. The great reformer of the kindred Persian branch of the Aryans could only solve the enigma by making evil (Ahriman), co-ordinate and nearly co-equal with good (Ormuzd). Gautama solved the question in another way; he simply ignored, and eliminated from his mind all idea of creating power, and then set to work to analyze the problems of existence, of good and of evil. The result he arrived at may be termed a "metaphysical natural development."

Though he silently ignores a creator in his teachings, he nowhere clearly denies him. It is said* that when one of his disciples asked him, "whether the existence of the world is eternal or not eternal," he made no answer; and the reason given is that it was not the practice of Buddha to reply to any question the purport of which was not designed in some way or other to assist in obtaining deliverance from successive existences, and attaining Nirvána. So the existence or non-existence of a creating Providence is omitted from his system, not necessarily as a falsity, but as a factor not required. He was too earnest and too wise to think he could proceed without a first cause, and in his search for this he elaborated the most wonderful ontological system ever conceived. He termed it the "circle of existences." In one point of view nothing can be simpler, in the other nothing more bewildering. The result of all his deep musings and intense mental struggles to arrive at the origin of evil and of all objective ideas, was to find the cause in "ignorance." Thence in natural order proceeded all else, thus:—

"On account of ignorance, merit and demerit are produced; on account of merit and demerit, consciousness; on account of consciousness, body and mind; on account of body and mind, the six organs of sense;† on account of the six organs of sense, contact (touch); on account of contact, desire; on account of desire,

* In the Malunka Sútra.

† The "mind" is the sixth sense.

sensation (pleasure or pain); on account of sensation, cleaving to existing objects; on account of clinging to existing objects, renewed existence (reproduction); on account of renewed existence, birth; on account of birth, decay, death, sorrow, misery (evil)." Thus we see all existence or being springs by means of ideas from "ignorance," and from existence (*per se*) arises all evil. This last thought is the keynote to the Buddhist religious system. But let us first examine the terms of this series of developments. Tracing it backwards we may readily admit the connection of each ascending term until we come to the first, "ignorance." What is ignorance? whence does it arise? what is its cause? To these questions we can find no answer. Ignorance is an abstract, *negative* term. The Pali word is *avijjâ* from *vijjâ* "knowledge," and *a* "not," privative; and its corresponding term is *moha* which the Buddhist doctors explain as "the spiritual ignorance which leads to a belief in the reality of external objects." This really seems to be nothing but the idealism of Berkeley, that "the fruitful source of all error was the unfounded belief in the reality and existence of the external world," that man can perceive nothing but his feelings and representations, and is the cause to himself of these. Berkeley's idealism led to a legitimate conclusion, the denial of the real existence of all external objects, while Gautama's landed him in the contradictory deduction that the "unfounded belief in the reality of external objects," led to the existence of those objects. If we may so express it, "negation," became a creative power, "*ex nihilo totum fit.*" This is the fundamental vice in the system evolved by Gautama; all his terms end in an undefined, and indefinable abstraction, and therefore, although he attributes the origin of all things to "ignorance," this itself has no prior term, and as it would be a senseless misuse of language to call it deity or creative power, it follows that really his system has no first cause, and is even less logical than the theory of the fortuitous combinations of atoms taught by the Atomic school. It is true that the Buddhist doctors allege that a *Buddha* alone can comprehend the manner in which the "ignorance," "merit," and "demerit" operate, and thus know how the circle of existence commenced. But in this they confess the fatal defect in their system, and seek to cover it by a foolish excuse. Neither Gautama himself nor his immediate disciples sought any such escape; they themselves doubtless did not perceive, the weak point in their teaching. In the famous Milinda-Prajna-Vastu (which contains one of the most scientific definitions of Buddhism), the Sage Nágasena, in order to explain his meaning, drew a perfect circle on the ground and asked the king if he could point out the beginning of it or the end. When the king confessed his inability, Nágasena said: "It is in this way that

Buddha propounded the 'circle of existence.'" And when the king again demanded to know what was the inherent inward life, or living principle, the sage again pointed to the circle, and repeated the formula, adding, "there is no such thing as the inward living principle of which you speak; besides that which is set forth in the 'circle of existence,' there is nought else."

But if the first terms in this circle were false, or at least incomplete, the after reasoning from them was logical enough. Since "existence" is the cause of all sorrow and all evil, the cessation of existence must necessarily be the means of relief. But how is that cessation to be obtained? Only by the cessation or destruction of the first term, "ignorance," and that is obtained by means of the acquirement of "knowledge." What knowledge? That of the only true science, my religion, says Gautama. And this consists in the knowledge of the unreality of all things, and of the sacred truth that only by the complete subjection of all thought, all desire, all sensation, can an escape from the misery of existence be obtained. In his great sermon or exposition of his creed to his disciples, Gautama says:—

"The sanctified disciple," having put restraint on (or conquered) the senses and their impressions, "puts restraint on the mind, and he puts restraint on objects of thought, and he puts restraint on thinking, and he puts restraint on mental impressions, and the effects of mental impressions, whether pleasure or pain, painless or pleasureless, whatever sensation is produced, on that also he puts restraint.

> "Having put on restraint, he is exempt from desire;
> He is liberated through absence from passion;
> Into 'liberation' he is liberated.—
> There is knowledge.—
> Birth is exhausted, religious duty is finished.
> That which ought to be done, has been done.
> Other things there are none."

Or, as it is expressed in a *sloka* or verse translated by Csoma de Körös:

> "No vice to be committed,
> Virtue perfectly to be practised;—
> Subdue entirely the thoughts.
> This is the doctrine of Buddha."

This religion then resolves itself into a system of the most absolute "quietism," and, as a natural consequence of its very existence, the most perfect and absolute morality. Everything depends on the entire and complete control or rather annihilation of the passions. This perhaps was also only what the Brahman hermits and sages sought to accomplish by means of their frightful and almost incredible penances and austerities. But Gautama set forth a different path towards that end. We have seen that his mind revolted against the existing Brahmanical system and and theory of penance; and so, as soon as he had arrived at the Buddhahood, that is at the final arrangement of his religious system, he makes his first public announcement of it thus: "There are two things ye should finally and for ever renounce—all worldly sources of pleasure and bodily gratification, and also excessive mortification of body, which neither tend to self-profit nor the profit of others.

> " Reject and forsake places and modes of excessive penance;
> Check and entirely control sensuous gratifications.
> If a man is able to follow these two lines of conduct,
> Immediately he will attain the trne way of eternal life."

It is true that Gautama instituted a monastic order, bound by the strictest rules on the minutest points; but this was not because he conceived there was any inherent merit or virtue in this state, but simply that the wise master clearly saw that no man, living in the ordinary outside world, could attain that state of philosophical abstraction, which was the absolute necessity of his system. The Buddhist monks are therefore *forbidden* to practice any useless austerities; they are commanded to do all that is necessary to preserve the body in health, but at the same time to think, "I do this not to please my appetite, but to satisfy the wants of nature."

The life of a recluse is not a means towards gaining superior merit, by self-sacrifice and mortification, as with the Brahman penitents, who sought to take heaven and the gods by storm, but an *assistance* to the weakness of human nature in seeking deliverance from the influence of all exterior objects of the senses. Certainly Gautama's teaching on the doctrine of abstinence and mastery of the passions, is the more manly, and more suited to the dignity of the human mind.

Having satisfied himself on all the points that had perplexed him, and constructed in his own mind the whole edifice of his new religion, or, in the language of his Buddhist followers, "having attained to the supreme wisdom of the Buddhahood," he began to teach, and to preach this new doctrine, the most wonderful, and to the multitude the most attractive, point in which must have been its spirit of universal brotherhood, and sympathy with suffering humanity. The wretched down-trodden Sudras, and the rich but despised Vaisyas (or merchants), with the proud Kshatriya Rajas chafing under the spiritual domination of an arrogant priesthood, had presented to them a religion which taught that they were the equals, in a spiritual sense, of the god-descended Brahman; that they needed not his mediation nor the practice of his complicated and wearisome rites to enable them to escape the consequences of their transgressions; a religion which attracted and won the best feelings of their nature by its mercifulness and abhorrence of cruelty and suffering, whether self-inflicted or imposed on others. What wonder that men, groaning under the intolerable burden of Brahmanical pride and gross and cruel superstitions, eagerly hailed this wonderful teacher as a saviour and deliverer? What wonder that grateful but ignorant crowds of disciples in after years surrounded the remarkable figure of the great prince-sage with a halo of marvel and mystery, such as we find in the Buddhist books? What wonder also, when we consider the simplicity of his *practical* moral doctrine, and the subtle and abstruse foundation of his philosophical teaching, that the more educated and refined minds of some of his followers, led thereto by the habits of abstraction and self-communing induced by monastic rule, gradually educed from the few propositions which formed the teachings of the founder of the religion, that exuberant and extraordinary maze of bewildering metaphysics that characterizes the later schools of Buddhist philosophy?

We have been endeavouring to present the idea of Gautama the *man,* not the mythical Buddha of five hundred fabled births, the great teacher and founder of a religion that belongs to one third part of the human race, divested of the absurd legends that have been attached to his name, in the same way as they have been in a less degree to that of a much later and more clearly historical teacher, Mahommed. There is little doubt that the want of a Deity or Providence in the system which Gautama expounded, is the chief reason why his own personality has become so confused and obscured; he supplies in the Buddhist religion that highest central position, which in almost every other faith Deity occupies, and thus all that craving for the marvellous and mysterious, which is so dear to the human instinct, centred in him.

Nevertheless, in spite of the indistinctness and the legendary absurdities which confuse and, as it were, blur the picture, Gautama stands out as the figure of one of the most wonderful religious reformers the world has seen—wonderful, not only from the results of his teachings, but even more so from that clear conception of virtue and moral rectitude which has induced good and even learned, though narrow-minded, men to ignore his individuality, and to seek in Buddhism a debased copy of Christianity. One more extract may be given in the ancient metrical form (gáthá), embodying a rule of life, the beauty of which all will admit.

A disciple inquires :—

> " By doing what, and observing what rules,
> And acquiring what ground of merit,
> May one attain an excellent condition as Deva or man,
> And so lay up in store future blessedness ? "

To this Gautama returned answer :—

> " Ministering to the worthy, doing harm to none,
> Always ready to render reverence to whom it is due,
> Loving righteousness and righteous conversation,
> Ever willing to listen to that which may profit another,
> Rejoicing to meditate on the true law,
> And to reflect on the words of Divine Wisdom,
> Practising every kind of self-discipline and pure life,
> Always doing good to those around you—
> This is, indeed, the wisdom of a good disciple."